The Devil Has No Mother

Also by Nicky Cruz

Run Baby Run
One Holy Fire: Let the Spirit Ignite Your Soul
Soul Obsession: Let God Set Your Heart on Fire

The Devil Has No Mother

Why He's Worse than You Think –
but God is Greater

Nicky Cruz

HODDER &
STOUGHTON

First published in Great Britain in 2012 by Hodder & Stoughton
An Hachette UK company

1

A CIP catalogue record for this title is available from the British Library

ISBN 978 1 444 70332 0

Typeset in Sabon MT by Hewer Text UK Ltd, Edinburgh

Printed and bound by CPI Group (UK) Ltd, Croydon, CR0 4YY

Hodder & Stoughton policy is to use papers that are natural, renewable and
recyclable products and made from wood grown in sustainable forests.
The logging and manufacturing processes are expected to conform
to the environmental regulations of the country of origin.

Hodder & Stoughton Ltd
338 Euston Road
London NW1 3BH

www.hodderfaith.com

A Special Dedication

*Even though you have ten thousand guardians in Christ,
you do not have many fathers, for in Christ Jesus I became
your father through the gospel. (1 Corinthians 4:15)*

I have been in love with Christ and serving him for many
years. Ironically, I have to say that the years have passed
by and though the snow has fallen on my hair, my spirit
is still young!

I can truly say that without the vision and obedience of
one particular man of God, I would not be here. More
than a half century ago, the Spirit of the Lord moved on
the heart of a man and woman in a little town in
Pennsylvania. David Wilkerson was possessed by a calling
and became pregnant with a vision from the Holy Spirit.
This vision and compassion pushed him into getting
involved with one of the most violent and hopeless eras of
the gang movement. It was as if he was being thrown into
a lion's den. I always wondered how this man could leave
his wife behind when she was expecting a baby at any time.
But the urging was so strong that Gwen, his beautiful wife,
released David to come to New York City with God's
message of hope and forgiveness. He took all of the hu-
miliation, rejection and punishment that I could throw at

him, and still he continued to park himself two inches from hell, and go out to fish for souls.

I knew David Wilkerson to be a man of courage and of faith. I am a witness that everything he touched in his ministry life was blessed by God. In their hearts and in their actions, David and Gwen were always the most giving and generous people that I know. They refused to be possessed by a name, or a reputation, or by success. Then, in the 1980s, David was again compelled to return to NYC to establish the Times Square Church smack in the heart of Babylon.

I will always be grateful to David and Gwen for helping me when I was in great need in my ministry, too. His ministry, World Challenge, continues to support Nicky Cruz Outreach to this day. Many people say that behind every great man of God is a great woman. I don't believe in that! The great woman is never behind the man; she stands beside him. Gwen Wilkerson is that great woman.

Some people thought that David and I went our separate ways over the years. That is not true – we remained close. In fact, we grew even closer in the last few years before his passing. He continued, to the end, to give me tremendous advice and speak into my life as a father.

For years, I have told people, and especially my family, that without David Wilkerson's obedience to go into the pits of hell, I wouldn't be here. Neither would millions of souls who have come to the Lord through Nicky Cruz Outreach, Teen Challenge and World Challenge. He told me that being in the ministry was rarely easy. One time I remember him telling me: 'Nicky, I sometimes get discouraged. When I do, I think of the day of your conversion and the miracle Jesus did in your life. Thinking of that day would lift my spirits and I could keep going. That memory always makes me happy.'

David had such a sensitive heart for the pain of others. History will tell of the legacy that he has left behind and the millions of people like me that he touched whom nobody else would have gotten close to. David told me one time that what a man does for Jesus is never in vain. I was always so proud of him when I heard him preach. He was an awesome preacher. He was right on in his discerning of the times. Whatever people say, I can say that I really knew him. Coming from my background, I lacked the influence and guidance of a father in my life. He was that and more to me.

During the more than two years that it took to write this book, I had the opportunity to speak to David about its progress and subject matter. I, like tens of thousands of others, was saddened and heartbroken when I heard of his death just hours after his fatal accident. This man, who became my mentor, left his heart in my heart and that's the reason I became an evangelist. Evangelism was the heart of David Wilkerson.

Son of God, husband, father, grandfather, evangelist, pastor, author, prophet, friend, confidant – my spiritual father and friend, David Wilkerson. The world has lost a truly great man.

Thank you again, David and Gwen, for loving my wife and children and for 'begetting me through the gospel' – I will be eternally grateful. Loving you both forever.

Nicky Cruz

Precious in the sight of the LORD *is the death of his saints.* (*Psalm 116:15*)

Contents

PART 1

Introduction

Be self-controlled and alert. Your enemy
the devil prowls around like a roaring lion
looking for someone to devour.

(1 Peter 5:8)

CHAPTER 1

Know Your Enemy

A call to the Church

On the afternoon of 5 February 2009, I was in Guatemala City, enjoying a meal with friends and colleagues at the home of Roberto Lopez, my spiritual son. We were rejoicing over what had happened the night before at the stadium where I had preached. Thousands had responded to the invitation to receive Jesus Christ, streaming down to the front from their seats all over the stadium. It was no wonder that, the next day, we were all in a light-hearted mood, laughing and talking loudly.

Then the phone rang. Pastor Bobby Cruz Jr (no blood relation to me) answered it and let me know that the call was from my home office in Colorado. Bobby started joking on the phone with my assistant, Karen Robinson, but then his face fell and he quickly carried the phone into another room.

Right then I knew something was wrong.

When Bobby came back a few minutes later, his face was grave. 'You'd better call your nephew Tato,' he told me. Tato is the son of my younger brother Rafael in Puerto Rico.

'Call my nephew? For what?' I asked. Then I started crying. 'Is my brother dead?' Rafael had recently undergone a heart operation, and I was sure he had died.

Bobby started crying too, and I could tell he was bursting to tell me the news he had been given. But as I found out later, Karen had emphasised with him that I should get the facts straight from my nephew, because the information she had received might not be accurate.

'Call Tato,' Bobby repeated.

So I did. It took a while to get through to my nephew, and in my heart I was already grieving Rafael; but when Tato finally came on the line, he said it was my older brother Frank who had died.

Frank had been murdered.

Martyr

Frank was four years older than me. He preceded me in moving to New York back in the 1950s, and it was his apartment I lived in when I first arrived in that city. He became a Christian not long after I did, going on to spend forty-two years as a pastor in New York and Puerto Rico. When he could have been retiring and taking it easy, he instead opened a rehab centre, Rock Christian Center, in our hometown of Las Piedras, Puerto Rico. He was very successful at weaning addicts off drugs and showing them a better way through Jesus.

As I learned, it was one of the addicts connected with the rehab centre who killed Frank. His name is Jomar Otero, and he was twenty-two at the time of the murder.

Some months earlier, Frank had tried to help Otero and had often spoken to him about the Lord. But the young man had dropped out of the drug addiction programme. Then, on the evening of 4 February, this young man suddenly showed up at the home of my brother and his wife, Mary. Otero said his car had run out of gas nearby.

Unbelievably, Otero spent a while sitting in Frank and Mary's home and talking with them about the Bible. There he was, with this terrible plan in his mind for Frank, and he was happily discussing Jesus with them! It reminds me of Judas sharing the Last Supper with the Lord.

Finally, Otero asked Frank to take him to get more gas. Mary warned Frank to be careful. The streets of their neighbourhood can be dangerous at night, and driving around with a young man like Otero wouldn't make them any less dangerous. But for most of his seventy-four years Frank had tried to help people and on this evening, the last of his life, he was still trying to help, thinking of others to his last breath.

What seems to have happened that night is this: Otero – perhaps with an accomplice, though none has yet been found – took Frank to a secluded location, beat him, then grabbed his belt and choked him to death with it. Then they threw his body in the trunk and used his car in a couple of robberies. They wanted to get hold of money to buy drugs.

Police found the car abandoned near a river early the next morning. My brother's body was still in the blood-soaked trunk, his face unrecognisable from the beating he'd taken as well as from the decomposition that was already underway in the intense Puerto Rican heat. It took forensic scientists to officially identify the body later that day. Only then did the awful news make its way to me in Guatemala via Colorado.

Was it necessary for Otero and whatever accomplice he may have had to kidnap my brother and kill him in order to carry out their robberies? Of course not. They could have stolen a car anywhere, with much less trouble and risk. Even if you take into account their drug-addled thinking, there is nothing reasonable about what they did. It's a sad truth, but the only reasonable explanation for my brother's brutal murder is this: *the devil deceived these young men into taking out this servant of God for him.*

Our family had turned our backs on the devil, whom we previously served. For many years, we had been doing our best to take ground from him for the sake of Christ. And so – without minimising the responsibility of the young men who committed the murder – I believe that my brother's death was a case of the devil lashing out at us. Unexpectedly. And oh so painfully.

A former gang member, I had flirted with danger and tempted death many times. I kept thinking that if a murder had to happen to anybody in the family, it should have been me, not Frank. It seemed incredible to me that my gentle, loving brother – the soft-spoken peacemaker in our family – would have his life ended for him like this, a casualty of spiritual and earthly violence. But it was true. It had really happened.

The press called my brother a martyr, and I believe they were right about that. He won many people to Christ in life, and he has won – and is still winning – more to Christ through his death. But this truth does only so much to make his loss easier to bear for those of us who loved him.

Dear, wonderful Frank. We played together as boys. We shared an apartment as young men. We served God side by side. We kept in touch down through the years, and our families remained close. He was my brother. And now he was gone.

Score one for the dark side.

Thirst for Revenge

Here's another sad truth. Evil is not only *out there*. It's also *in here*. It's in our hearts. Even when we have been redeemed, our sinful nature is all too ready to co-operate with any scheme the devil might have up his sleeve. I was reminded of this truth when I returned to Puerto Rico later in the year to attend the court hearing for my brother's killer.

While violence is common in my beloved homeland of Puerto Rico, the killing of an old man and a pastor outraged the community. The mayor himself got involved in expediting efforts to find the killer. And it wasn't long before Jomar Otero was taken into custody and brought to trial. (His accomplice, if indeed there was one, has not yet been brought to justice.)

And now I must confess to you that, before the hearing, I was struggling mightily with my sinful nature. The pain of my grief was unbelievable, almost unbearable. It hurt so much! And not surprisingly, I couldn't sleep the night before the hearing. If it had been the old days – my gang days – I could have killed Otero without thinking twice about it. Now, I couldn't seriously think about taking such extreme measures. But I *was* struggling with my human nature, feeling hate and wanting deep inside to get some kind of revenge. Thankfully, though, Jesus has control of our human nature!

The next morning, I fell into the arms of my nephew Tato and told him about the thoughts of revenge going through my mind. Three years earlier, God had used me in bringing Tato to faith (a story to be told in a future chapter). And now Tato was saying to me, 'Uncle, you cannot do this. You have too much to lose. You have a God of justice. You have your family and your reputation. You must forgive.'

I knew he was right. I have often preached that, when you have been hurt by others, forgiveness is a choice you have to make, for your own spiritual well-being. And when we forgive, we give up our right to hurt somebody. We cannot retaliate.

Not long after, I admitted to interviewers from the secular media in Puerto Rico that I had been seriously considering how I could harm the man who had murdered my brother. But I also told them that, on the day I talked to Tato, I forgave Jomar Otero. And in fact, the same is true for everyone in my family – Frank's widow, my other brothers, my sister, my nephews and nieces, all of us. We have all forgiven this young man. This testimony on TV made a big impact throughout Puerto Rico.

The judge ordered Otero to life in prison without the possibility of parole. He is in isolation so that none of the other prisoners will kill him for murdering a community leader. If I get a chance to speak to Jomar in prison (and I hope I do), I will tell him that I forgive him. And I will tell him that Jesus wants to forgive him too. It's what Frank would want.

So, no, I'm not going to take revenge against my brother's killer. But that doesn't mean I'm not going to strike back against the real enemy. And who is that, again? The apostle Paul said it: 'For our struggle is not against flesh and blood, but against the rulers, against the authorities, against the powers of this dark world and against the spiritual forces of evil in the heavenly realms.'[1]

My brother's blood cries out to me to tell the world about the danger of the evil that's afoot in the world. In fact, the blood of *all* those harmed by Satan and his demons cries out for the truth to be known.

Satan must be unmasked. He is not a harmless caricature or a myth left over from humanity's primitive past. He's not a symbol of human wrongdoing. He's not the personification of some generalised force. He's a real being – and the most awful one we could imagine. And he is a hopeless case.

The Devil Has No Mother

There is an old Spanish saying that I remember well from my days as a child in Puerto Rico. It's something that adults would often say when referring to a boy who seemed bent on evil and destruction – a child who lived in rebellion against authority. People would say, *'Ese hombre no tiene madre.'* Translated, this phrase means, 'This guy has no mother.' I remember the phrase well . . . because adults would often use it when referring to me. *I* was a lost case!

When I was a young man, my heart was filled with evil and rebellion. I ran amok in the streets of Las Piedras and then New York, looking for trouble and finding it around every corner. I was bent on destruction, constantly revolting against authority. And I knew what the people of my neighbourhood thought of me – I could see the disdain in their eyes. To my face, they cowered in fear. But behind my back, they whispered among themselves, *'Ese hombre no tiene madre.'* I was like a child who had no mother.

The devil has that same problem: he's hopeless. He lacks any soft spot. He roams the earth with nothing but hate in his heart, despising all that is good and wholesome, scheming to warp and destroy everything that God has made. His being is rotten to the core.

This is our true enemy.

Ese hombre no tiene madre.

My friend, none of us is safe from attack by the devil and his forces. And it's time we realised it.

Battle Cry

I've been an evangelist for many years now. Over that time, by God's grace, I've visited numerous countries, travelled hundreds of thousands of miles and spoken before millions of people. And as you might guess, I've noticed many changes taking place.

One of the most disturbing trends I've noticed within the Church in recent years is a growing blindness towards the reality of the devil and the enormity of the threat he poses. It seems that many of us have forgotten that we've got an enemy, one who hates us and would love to see us destroyed.

Paul said that he and other early Christians would not be outwitted by the devil, because they were 'not unaware of his schemes'.[2] But that's no longer true of us. We *are* unaware. We're focused on our own problems, and on wars taking place in spots like Iraq and Afghanistan, but we've forgotten the more important war that's going on in the spiritual realm. Mesmerised by world events and personal sagas, we're desensitised to the devil. And as a result, we're apathetic. Distracted. Naive. Gullible. Hardly a threat to the devil and his wicked plans.

This book is a message – no, a shout – to the Church: *Wake up!* The devil is real and active in this world, and we'd better understand what he's doing before it's too late. We need a knowledge of his power, as well as of the even greater power for good that is available to us, if we are to serve God faithfully as soldiers in the spiritual war that's going on. And if we don't regain that knowledge in time, then I fear that the devil may take control all over the world. He's gone far enough as it is.

In this book we'll take a deep and honest look into the tactics of the devil and see how evil works. I'm not the ultimate authority on the subject, but I've had more experience with the evil one than most, and I feel called to warn and educate the body of believers. Because of that, I plan to pull no punches. I'm going to be completely honest and transparent with you regarding the things I've seen and experienced. It's information you've got to have.

Maybe you've heard accusing words in your mind.

Maybe you've struggled again and again with temptation.

Maybe you've been gullible to devilish lies.

Maybe you've seen disturbing manifestations of evil.

Maybe you're just aware that you need to know more about this topic of the devil.

Whatever your experiences relating to personal evil, this book will explain to you what it means – and what you can do about it.

I wish I could tell you that, if you will read this book, you will be able to escape all the devil's attacks and live in blissful freedom from harm. But it doesn't work that way. Such bliss is to come for us only in heaven. In this world there is no place to run away from the spiritual war that's taking place. There are no non-combatants, whether you are a believer or not.

But I *can* assure you that knowing the threat that faces you will make you better prepared to fight. In *The Devil Has No Mother* you will learn the limitations of the devil's influence. You will gain confidence in the Lord's ability to defeat evil. And you will learn how to take up the weapons God gives you to fight in his name.

Some of the stories you are about to read about the devil may make you uncomfortable; they may even scare you. But I encourage you to stay with me. Don't stop reading. This is a message God wants you to hear.

Also, keep in mind that we're not just going to talk about the devil; we're also going to discuss God's magnificent glory and some of the incredible things he has done – in my life and in the lives of others. You'll be both informed and encouraged by these stories. The overriding message of this book is one of confidence and reassurance. The devil has no mother, but we have a heavenly Father who gives us the victory as we continue to trust in him.

As you read, please know that I've already been in prayer for you, your family and your walk with God. I've prayed that he will reveal his power in you. Therefore I'm confident that, as you call on the name of Jesus Christ and the power in his blood, the demons will tremble before you. And God will receive all the glory.

Now it's time to move on. We have to understand more about our enemy. Who is the devil? Where did he come from? How did he get to this 'motherless' state, the central player and chief instigator of evil?

For those answers, we must go back in time – back even before the creation of the earth. Back to the origin of the spiritual conflict that has since caught up my brother Frank, me . . . and you.

CHAPTER 2

Dragon's Fury

How the evil one got that way

His name was Lucifer. One of God's most powerful and glorious creations. Beloved and honoured among the heavenly hosts. Full of light. Anointed cherub, charged to protect the holy mount of God.

Lucifer reigned supreme among the angels, stood exalted in the universe as a model of perfection, full of wisdom and perfect in beauty. Adorned with every precious stone conceived by God: ruby, topaz, emerald, chrysolite, onyx, jasper, sapphire, turquoise and beryl. His jewellery was mounted in pure gold, prepared for him on the morning of his creation. God loved Lucifer even before he was created, like a father loves a son.

Heaven gasped in wonder as God breathed life into Lucifer's chest, as his mighty wings twitched and unfolded, as God's most magnificent creation came to life. God smiled as his beloved angel danced among the clouds, lighting the heights of heaven with his splendour.

Lucifer would reign at the head of God's creation. He would stand guard over heaven and earth, command legions of angels in worship to God, bow only to the holy Trinity. Even Gabriel and Michael let Lucifer lead them in the celestial chorus.

In the beginning, Lucifer loved God freely. Like all of God's creations, Lucifer was born with a mind that reasoned without restraint. The words of worship on his lips were his own. His love and loyalty to God were voluntary. He loved God out of desire, not obligation.

Heaven was at peace, living in harmony before the great and masterful Creator.

A shadow lengthens in heaven

But one day something began to stir deep within the chief among angels. Something sinister, dark and forbidden. Feelings he shouldn't be feeling. Thoughts he shouldn't be thinking.

Lucifer was jealous.

During times of worship, Lucifer's lips would shower God with praise. Standing at the head of creation, his hands would raise in reverence. His knees would bow in humility before the Almighty. But deep in his gut, envy was simmering. His love was turning to spite. Affection was transforming into anger. Adoration was giving way to pride and arrogance.

Lucifer might still be walking before God's throne, fulfilling the purpose for which God created him, if only he had reined in the envious desires within him. If only he had been able to overcome the evil thoughts that stirred. *If only he had gone before God in repentance, asking for help, instead of longing to possess God's throne. If only he had let his jealousy go.*

But he didn't. In the end, Lucifer gave in to the pride swelling within his being. 'I will ascend to heaven,' said Lucifer. 'I will raise my throne above the stars of God; I will sit enthroned on the mount of assembly, on the utmost heights of the sacred mountain. I will ascend above the tops of the clouds; I will make myself like the Most High.'

Lucifer's envy was no longer contained. For the first time in the history of creation the heavens prepared for conflict. Because God's chosen angel was intent on living for himself rather than for God.

Leaving God's sanctuary, Lucifer set out to incite dissatisfaction and mutiny among the celestial beings. He whispered and schemed, darting through the halls of heaven, stirring rebellion. 'Follow me,' he told those who would listen, 'and I will make you great and mighty among all creatures. Bow before Lucifer and you will reign beside me. The throne of heaven will soon be mine, and in that day I will not forget your allegiance.'

The one who once summoned creation to worship its Creator now sought that worship for himself. The one who once shone with the light of God's splendour and grace now flickered uncertainly, flirting with revolt.

Lucifer's silver tongue soon gained a mighty following. A third of all God's angels turned their devotion away from their Creator and took up a sword beside Lucifer. His lies of passion and flattery soon darkened legions of hearts within the celestial realm. His army was poised for battle.

Lucifer the blameless one, the glorious cherub of God, had now become Lucifer the Dragon. Now there was no turning back. Creation was at war.

The banishment

Michael took up a sword against the great Lucifer, summoning angels from the four corners of the universe to defend the mount of God. The Dragon and his mutinous army fought back with fury. All across the heavens the battle raged as angels and archangels, celestials of all types, drew back swords and arrows against the Dragon's insurgent armies.

In the end, the Dragon's forces were no match for God's mighty army. Heaven held its ground against Lucifer's fury. The victory went to Michael.

Michael bound the Dragon's hands and wings, stripping him of the gold and jewels that adorned him. In place of beauty, there was only blackness. Satan's pride had turned his soul to ashes. So God commanded Michael to banish Lucifer from the heavenly realms. 'Seize the Great Dragon and his legions of darkness and hurl them to the earth,' he said. 'There they will remain, until the last day, when they will burn in the lake of fire. No more will Lucifer shine in heaven. No more will he serve at the foot of my throne. No more will he be called an archangel of God, but "Satan", the adversary. The deceiver. The sworn enemy of love and goodness. The prince of corruption will reign no more in my presence!'

So Michael did as God commanded. He hurled Satan to the earth, his fallen angels plummeting all around him. The once-glorious Lucifer now slithered on his belly in shame. The cherub of light was now the dark prince of earth. Satan the accuser, the doomed dragon of pride and deceit and turmoil, the enemy of God, now had a new throne – the throne of darkness.

Heaven was once more at peace. But the universal battle for human souls had just begun.

> *Woe to the earth and the sea,*
> *because the devil has gone down to you!*
> *He is filled with fury,*
> *because he knows that his time is short.*

Lucifer Unleashed

Much of the account above is speculation, of course, an attempt to frame what might have happened in heaven as Lucifer rebelled.[1] Many of the details of Satan's rebellion will likely remain a mystery to us this side of heaven. God created Lucifer to love him freely, just as he desires you and me to do, but Lucifer rejected him. The strengths that God lavished on him became for him a source of pride, leading to his downfall.

He is described with thirty-three titles in the Old Testament and thirteen in the New Testament, including 'the god of this age', 'the prince of this world', 'the evil one', 'the father of lies', the one 'who leads the whole world astray', the 'accuser', 'the ruler of the kingdom of the air', 'enemy' and 'serpent'. His titles are as plentiful as his hate for humankind. And he has only one agenda: 'to steal and kill and destroy' everything that God has created.[2]

Ephesians 6:12 suggests that Satan has several layers of evil forces serving under his command, carrying out his bidding, wreaking havoc upon the earth. How many demons serve him has not been told to us, but Scripture implies that 'legions' of angels were cast down with him – perhaps a full third of all the angels in heaven.[3]

We also don't know just how much power and leverage God allows Satan and his demons to have, only that his methods of deception have turned many hearts away from their Creator. The Liar is a master of lies, and his tricks have proven very effective.

But for all we don't know about the fall of Satan, there is one thing we do know. God has chosen to use the human race – you and me – as vital players in his plan to advance his kingdom in heaven and earth, and Lucifer is just a pawn in that plan. The end of the story has already been written. Satan is a defeated foe, though still actively plotting to thwart God's final plan, until he will meet his inevitable demise in the lake of fire.[4] Like a caged animal on its way to slaughter, he scratches and yells and fights for freedom, but he will never gain it. He has no hope of surviving God's ultimate plan of redemption for humankind.

Yet still he fights. Still he struggles to overcome. Still he wars against God and God's creation. Still he labours daily to persuade us of his power, to deceive humanity into believing he is somehow equal with God. The deceiver can't touch God, so he attacks those who were made in

God's image – you and me. He can't win, but he has pledged to scrap and claw till his last breath. And humankind is caught in the middle.

Taking Authority

So, where does that leave us? Are we doomed to suffer damage from the forces of evil arrayed against us? Far from it.

Now I'm going to tell you something extraordinary, something you might have a hard time believing: *We, as children of God, have authority over Satan.* It's incredible but true. Paul said, 'The God of peace will soon crush Satan under your feet.' James said, 'Resist the devil, and he will flee from you.'[5] And they meant it. We really do have such authority over the devil and his evil spirits.

It's not because we are powerful in ourselves. The truth is, Satan is much more powerful than we are. Our fighting him in our own strength would be like a ninety-nine-pound weakling putting up his fists to fight the heavyweight boxing champ of the world. But as much as Satan is stronger than we are, so God is far, far stronger than Satan is.[6] And it is God's power we use to defeat the devil.

Jesus said, 'All authority in heaven and on earth has been given to me.'[7] And he passed that authority on to us – to those who follow him. When he walked the earth two thousand years ago, he specifically gave his disciples authority over evil spirits.[8] He gives the same authority to all of us who believe in and walk with him.

Listen to this and believe it, because it is the scriptural truth: we are the Church of Jesus Christ, and the gates of

Hades will not stand against us, because we have been given the keys of the kingdom. Through the delegated authority of Christ, what we bind on earth will be bound in heaven and what we loose on earth will be loosed in heaven.[9]

Like in the days of Jesus Christ, we find ourselves in a mix of trouble. It includes poverty, pornography, drug use, child abuse, adultery, murder, rape and Christians struggling with their faith. There is no cure for all cancers and illnesses, but God does heal. Problems exist, but people are not defenceless, without the power to fight. We have no reason to fear Satan and his demons.

Through Jesus, you and I have complete authority over evil and sin. God has given us power over darkness, power to overcome our sinful nature, power to move mountains – those obstacles that block our sight to the wondrous working of God – in the name of Jesus. Power far greater than most of us realise. Weak in ourselves, we are mighty through God. Satan and the evil spirits tremble at the thought that we might recognise our authority and use it!

Jesus urged us to be as 'wise as serpents', because after all that's the only way to stand up against the Great Serpent, Lucifer.[10] So let's do that. Let's learn what we're up against and what we can do about it. In the next set of chapters we'll be looking at key ways the devil attacks.

PART 2

The Devil

[The devil] was a murderer from the beginning, not holding to the truth, for there is no truth in him. When he lies, he speaks his native language, for he is a liar and the father of lies.

(John 8:44)

CHAPTER 3

The Beast is Loose

The universal conflict comes home

I've spent most of my adult life warning people against the deceiver's lies and tricks, and because of it, our family has been under constant spiritual attack. We've experienced the devil's wrath more than most families could comprehend. We've never feared him, but we've also learned not to underestimate the extent of his hatred. We know the chaos he is capable of inflicting upon an unsuspecting world, and he knows we will do everything in our power to stop him. Because of that truth, we've witnessed more than our share of evil.

Just a few years ago, our family was once again touched by evil in a way that still sends chills down my spine whenever it comes to mind. It was an event that made news headlines throughout the world and forever impacted the lives of many people, including my two oldest grandchildren.

Looking into the Eyes of Evil

It happened on 9 December 2007, at New Life Church in Colorado Springs, Colorado. New Life was the home congregation for my daughter Alicia and her husband, Patrick, along with their two children, Isabella and Nikolas. At the time, Isabella was seventeen and Nikolas was fourteen.

Following an uplifting Sunday morning service, a gunman suddenly opened fire in the middle of the parking lot. Dozens of people were standing nearby as bullets flew in every direction. Isabella and Nikolas were sitting in the family car just a few yards away from the gunman, Matthew Murray. They froze in fear as the deranged young man fired one shot after another randomly towards the playground. Right in front of their eyes, he killed two beautiful young girls at point-blank range, Rachel and Stephanie Works. He shot them down like deer. Isabella locked eyes with the gunman as the two young girls fell to their deaths. She sat petrified as Murray turned and pointed his gun directly at her and Nikolas. They were clearly his next targets.

At that moment another car drove directly past them. In a split second, that car distracted the gunman, and he instead turned his weapon toward the passing car, shattering the back window. Isabella quickly put her car into gear and sped away in the opposite direction, barely escaping the bullets.

Thankfully, my grandchildren were safe. But the ordeal was not yet over. The young man reloaded his weapons and burst through the side door of the church building, where he sprayed bullets into the foyer that just minutes before had been full of churchgoers. Thanks to the bravery of a church security guard, he was stopped in his tracks in the middle of the hallway and lay bleeding and helpless. He eventually turned his gun on himself.

During the entire ordeal, Patrick and Alicia were in the church's chapel waiting to attend a reception for Dr Jack Hayford, who was the visiting pastor that day. They had heard the shots fired but had no idea their kids were in peril.

It was later discovered that Murray had set out the night before on his killing spree, specifically targeting Christians as his victims. In Denver he had shot and killed two young people on the campus of Youth With A Mission, who had expelled him from a missionary training programme. After going to the YWAM facility, he went home and rested for a while, plotting his next move. What kind of a person could lie down and rest after killing and wounding innocent people? Perhaps the kind of person who is possessed by evil.

The next day, Matthew headed to Colorado Springs to continue his rampage at the New Life Church campus. Now, it was cold, snowy and icy that Sunday, and I can't help but wonder if those conditions delayed him. Certainly if he had arrived earlier, more people would have been inside the church or going to their cars. The casualty figures might have been far higher. So it must have been the providence of God that slowed him down that day. Nevertheless, while worship was going on inside the New Life auditorium, a killer was on his way.

He killed four people and wounded several others before being taken down by the New Life security guard. I shudder to imagine how many more innocent people might have lost their lives if it had not been for the quick action taken by the New Life security team.

My grandchildren stared into the cold, dark eyes of evil that day. It was like the devil was trying to scar their minds with horror. Knowing this, Gloria and I convinced the family to stay with us for several days so that we could minister to them. When they arrived at our house we were so concerned seeing how traumatised they were. Particularly Isabella, who had a blank, cold stare. So we supported each other and prayed together to the One who sustains all things by his powerful word.[1]

My two precious grandchildren witnessed something I've seen far too many times in my life. They saw the hopelessness and rage of a person held captive to the enemy's lies. They saw the wrath of a man gone insane with envy and hate. A man who allowed his heart to be rotted to the core with the jealousy of the evil serpent.

They saw what God saw in the heart of Lucifer as he rebelled against the heavenly throne so many ages ago.

Our Times

You and I are living in evil times. There's no other way to describe it. We're living under a dark cloud of sin and despair and spiritual apathy.

It seems that each passing week brings more tragedy. Young people don't feel safe on school campuses for fear of another shooting or act of terrorism. The Internet has ushered them into a world of sin and sex and all kinds of illicit images. Because of it, parents are forced to be more vigilant than ever. We have to supervise our kids in a way that our parents could never have imagined doing.

Recently I heard of a phenomenon circulating the Internet called 'The Blasphemy Challenge'. It's a movement among youth and young adults where they encourage each other to record a message damning themselves to hell. Then, once the recording is made, it is posted on the Internet for other kids to watch. The instructions say, 'You may damn yourself to hell however you like, but somewhere in the video you must say the phrase "I deny the Holy Spirit."'

Whoever came up with this statement obviously understood the supernatural world and had a working knowledge of the Bible. In the Gospel of Mark, God distinctly warns of the dangers of this statement: 'Whoever blasphemes against the Holy Spirit will never be forgiven; he is guilty of an eternal sin.'[2]

Blasphemy of the Holy Spirit is when you know for certain that a miracle of God that involves the Holy Spirit is done and you deny it and give credit to the devil instead. It is a dangerous offence and should never be taken lightly, even in jest. This is no joke and it's not a game. Cursing the Holy Spirit is a serious offence and a direct affront to the holiness of God.

For centuries, Christians have faced the constant threat of persecution, confiscation of property, even martyrdom. But we are not used to this in my home country, the United States, or in other parts of the West. We talk about blessing and prosperity and God's goodness, all of which are true.

But we need to remember that nowhere in Scripture are we promised a life free of conflict and suffering. In fact, Jesus tells us that his followers will be hated just as he was hated.[3]

'Be very careful, then, how you live – not as unwise but as wise, making the most of every opportunity, because the days are evil,' wrote Paul.[4] And that message is more pertinent today than at any time in living memory. Some important wisdom about spiritual warfare is exactly what I'm aiming to give you in this book.

And the first thing we need to do in combating our enemy is to realise that he's at work in our land, in our day. We need to open our eyes: evil is all around. It's not just somewhere far away. It's right at hand. And it's not getting better. If anything, it's getting worse. The sooner we wake up to it, the better we'll be able to deal with it.

An Angry Foe

If you have read my autobiography, *Run Baby Run*, then you know about my early years. I grew up in Puerto Rico, one of nineteen children, in a home with parents who were practising spiritists. I moved to New York as a teen and quickly became warlord of one of the most vicious gangs in the city, the Mau Maus. I was involved in the gang's lifestyle of drug use, casual sex, theft, intimidation, fighting and even killing. But that all changed when a pastor named David Wilkerson dared to come onto our turf and tell us about Jesus. My life was changed forever when I received Christ as my personal Saviour, and I went on to study at Bible college and become an evangelist.

What you probably don't know is the larger story of my involvement with evil forces, from early childhood and throughout the decades of my adult life. That's what I'll be telling, anecdote by anecdote, as future chapters in this book unfold. At first I was a helpless victim and plaything of demons. Then I became their opponent, determined to defeat them whenever I could. And because of all this, it's become plain to me that the world we live in is not as safe as we would like to think.

Lucifer's first attack on the human race, after being banished to the earth, began as early as the Garden of Eden. He sneaked up on the first woman, Eve, and persuaded her to eat the fruit that God had put off limits. Her sin and Adam's has tainted all of their children ever since. If you need proof, consider how the first murder was committed between the very first generation of their offspring![5]

It was no random chance that caused the first family to be the devil's first target. Think about it. Jesus had a wonderful mother who loved and nurtured him as he grew – Mary. Most of us, thankfully, likewise had loving mothers. But the devil had no mother and is devoid of love. He particularly hates families. And that's why he went after Eve, the mother of the first family. Today, likewise, he hates the family and constantly attacks the family unit.

The devil has been doing his best to follow up his early success with more harm to the human race. And in every generation he's been successful. Every generation faces his temptation, his affliction, his deception. Who are we to think we might escape?

I am convinced that the enemy of our souls has launched an all-out assault on the Body of Christ. He is directing an angry and violent wave of hopelessness and despair, attacking our lives, families and finances. I am equally convinced that God, in his infinite love and mercy, is pruning and purging his Body in order to strengthen us and to prepare us for growth and fruitfulness. He is making us distinct, set apart, different. We have got to learn to co-operate with what he is doing and not give aid and comfort to the enemy.

When teaching his disciples how to pray, Jesus instructed them to say, 'Lead us not into temptation, but deliver us from the evil one.'[6] Jesus understood that, in order to overcome evil in evil times, good people must steer clear of sin and deception. We cannot allow ourselves to be desensitised to sin or to overlook the power of the evil one to lead us astray. We cannot let our guard down, even for an instant. And as we activate the authority Christ gives us, we *will* be delivered from evil.

We Shall Overcome

The shooting at New Life Church was just one of Satan's many attempts to destroy this powerful community of believers. A year earlier he had succeeded in seducing and bringing down the ministry of Ted Haggard, the church's founding pastor. And now the evil one had come back for another round of chaos, now with the church under the leadership of Pastor Brady Boyd. But Pastor Brady knows the enemy's tricks and wasn't about to fall for them.

On the Wednesday following the horrible attack, Pastor Brady called for a congregational meeting. He took to the pulpit and – with the media cameras rolling and the entire world listening in – declared to the congregation, 'We will not be ruled by fear!' At that instant the church took to their feet to join him in this proclamation. The statement made front-page headlines in the local paper and has since become a declaration of defiance for the entire congregation. *We will not be ruled by fear!*

And they have not forgotten that promise. I've been to the church a number of times since that day, and I've spoken to the congregation, and today they are as strong and powerful a force for good as any church I've seen. Under the leadership of Pastor Brady and many others on staff, the church has continued to move forward and carry out the vision that God has given them.

Yes, evil is a present reality for every one of us. But the message Jesus wants us to hear is that overcoming evil is possible with God's help. We have every reason to cry, 'We will not be ruled by fear!' We are more than conquerors through him who loved us, and the demons can do nothing to separate us from the love of God in Christ Jesus our Lord.[7]

CHAPTER 4

Dabbling with Danger

Gateways to the demonic

I see a level of naivety today within the body of believers that astounds me. Christians are getting involved with devilish things as I never would have imagined thirty or forty years ago. Teens watch TV shows and movies with names like *Ghost Whisperer*, *Medium*, *The Vampire Diaries*, *True Blood*, *Psychic Kids* and *Paranormal State*. Some teens love horror movies, play violent video games and dress in the death-mimicking Goth style. Others who are into heavy metal music flash the 'cornuto', a hand signal representing horns that is an ancient Satanist symbol. I see kids mimicking the spells they find in the Harry Potter books. Grown-ups read *The Da Vinci Code* (rewriting Jesus' history) and *The Secret* (teaching that we can fulfil our selfish wishes through mind power). They go to tarot card readings and rearrange their home decoration according to the Chinese religious principles in feng shui.

I'm not talking about non-Christians doing these things. I'm talking about Christians doing them! And what they're not recognising is that, as they foolishly play around with ungodly practices or forms of entertainment, they are opening themselves up to demonic influence. These things can be gateways to still worse evil.

But wait – is watching a vampire show on TV or reading a novel like *The Da Vinci Code* really all that serious? Well, if you've ever done such a thing, I hope you'll escape harm from it. But I very much worry that it could be a step towards dishonouring your faith in God. People really have gone from dressing Goth to committing suicide, from trying out tarot to using a medium to contact the dead. And the devil and his demons are eager to conduct any of us down that road.

Of course, there have always been people who have dabbled in things they shouldn't have. Remember King Saul and his visit to the witch of Endor?[1] But in recent years such things have gotten noticeably more common within the Church. I've watched the trend with deep concern. A lack of seriousness about these gateway behaviours goes right along with our loss of urgent awareness about the devil.

Perhaps I would not be so disturbed by this trend if I did not know from personal experience just how dangerous dabbling in the demonic can be, especially for the young.

A 'Healing Spirit'

When I was growing up in Puerto Rico, my parents were deeply involved in witchcraft, summoning spirits of the dead, casting spells, healing through the help of spirits, foretelling the future and practising any other form of 'white magic' they could think of. They were naive enough to think that the 'good spirits' they summoned were from God, but that was because they had so little understanding of such things. They only saw the power that it brought, not the source.

I remember watching a man from our village come walking down the road to our house. He worked on a sugar plantation near Humaçao, Puerto Rico, just a few miles away. As he approached, I could see how pale and skinny he was. His eyes seemed vacant and listless. And his skin was greenish yellow. He looked like a corpse.

My father met him at the door and asked what was wrong. 'I've been feeling sick for two months,' he said, 'and the doctor can't find anything wrong with me. He says I am going to die, but he doesn't know why. Nothing he does seems to help.'

The man had come to our house because he'd heard of Papa's healing powers and was desperate to get well. Papa smiled and brought him into the Spirit House (the small building back of our house where my parents conducted their sorcery) and then sent one of my brothers to fetch Mama. I watched through a small window as they began their ceremony, wanting to get a look but not wanting to venture too close.

From the window I saw Papa begin his healing ritual, chanting, mixing things, raising his hands, closing his eyes, calling on the spirit world for help. Suddenly Mama jolted in her chair. And her face began to change. Her cheeks and mouth began to contort, as if she were taking on the shape of the sick man. She almost looked like him. And her skin began to turn the same colour – a yellowish green. I wanted to run in and help her, but I was afraid. I knew that this was part of their healing ceremony, having seen it before, but I could never get used to it.

Papa often said that, in order to heal, Mama would sometimes have to take on the sick person's affliction, so that they would know what to do. The evil spirits would enter Mama's body, and then he would know how to rid her of them. He said that Mama had the power to ward off spirits when others could not. Otherwise the 'good spirits' wouldn't be able to help them.

On this day, Mama continued to shake and shudder, continued to turn yellow and green, to change and contort, until finally Papa said to the man, 'Now I know what is wrong. Someone has placed an evil curse on you, someone who wants to hurt you. Go back to your home and dig beneath the north-east corner of your house. There you will find seven chicken bones tied to a coffin nail. Burn it all in a fire so hot that the nails melt, until it is completely gone. Then the curse that has been put upon you will be destroyed.'

The man found the chicken bones tied to a coffin nail just where Papa said he would. He immediately followed Papa's orders and burned the whole thing up. Two days later he came back to our house, healthy and spry. The sickness was gone. He all but skipped down the road to our home. This time he had a goat with him, which he offered to Papa as payment for saving his life.

Proof of Power

Such occurrences were so common that I can't even recall most of the healings that Papa did. It became a normal part of growing up in the Cruz household. Though I didn't know then how God stands against any involvement in the occult, I never liked what went on in the Spirit House.[2] I never could get used to seeing my mama channel spirits and take on sicknesses and foretell the future, and I felt suspicious of their religion.

More than that, when I was a young boy, evil spirits frightened me relentlessly. I have vivid memories of the demonic beings that would visit my room at night. They would come when I least expected them, when I wasn't ready, and toy with me, play with my mind. I saw things in the room, strange things moving about, shaking the curtains, darting through the shadows. And there were voices. Sometimes they would leave; other times they would remain throughout the night, keeping me shuddering beneath the covers. Many times the spirits would cross over into the physical world and hold me down on my bed. Before I could flee, they would pounce on me, putting their full weight on my small body. It felt like a two-hundred-pound man was lying on top of me, pressing me onto my mattress. I couldn't breathe or speak, couldn't yell, couldn't even move. I was helpless. I would start to cry, begging them in my mind to leave me alone, but they only pressed harder. This sometimes went on for hours at a time. Then suddenly they would lift and leave as quickly as they came. Perhaps the demons tired of taunting me, so they moved on to look for another victim, such as one of my brothers or my sister.

When I told my papa about these things, I could tell he didn't believe me. He told me how he and Mama had taken care to protect our family from evil spirits, that only good spirits surrounded our home. But even as a child I knew better. Something was definitely not right.

Years later, the Cruz relatives came together and recognised the many curses against us as a family – the curses of adultery, drunkenness, violence and more. We humbled ourselves and went to God for his protection. All my family are in a much better place, spiritually, now. But for a long time we were all open to evil influence because of what our parents had done.

Atheism for Children

You might say that your family is nothing like mine, that you never summon spirits. And I hope you don't! But are there other, more subtle ways in which you are dabbling in danger? Things like the examples I gave at the beginning of this chapter? Perhaps movies or TV shows you watch. Or books you read.

Let me give one example of a book series that many parents, even Christian parents, are letting their children read. It's the trilogy *His Dark Materials* (comprising *Northern Lights*, *The Subtle Knife* and *The Amber Spyglass*) by author Philip Pullman. I want to demonstrate to you how dangerous even a seemingly innocent children's book can be.

What's not to like about an adventure book series that features children, animals and exciting travel? Well, for one thing, Pullman – an avowed atheist – has openly admitted that his goal with these books and the associated movies is to destroy God in the minds of children. The theme of the series is that God and the Church are overbearing authorities (God is called 'the Authority' and the Church is 'the Magisterium'), who hunt down and torture children, and that they must be resisted and overthrown.

Included in the books' themes are the following ideas: the fall of humanity is a good thing because independence from an 'Authority' is to be commended, not punished; God and the Church are dangerous entities seeking to control and separate people from their souls; and the best thing that children can do is ignore these authorities, including parents, and think for themselves. Pullman rejects the 'Kingdom of Heaven' and would substitute for it the 'Republic of Heaven', where the 'Authority' (God) is dead.

Space does not permit me to go on with the appalling messages from Pullman's philosophy, but you get the idea. While some will dismiss the books and movies as harmless fantasy, they are anything but that. We are told in Scripture to guard our hearts with all diligence, and that includes the impressionable hearts of the children who are entrusted to our care.[3] Planting seeds of doubt and resentment towards God will at some point bear poisonous fruit in the life of a child, and I would beg you to protect your children from this poison, even if they feel they are 'the only ones' who haven't seen the movie or read the book. May God give us the wisdom and strength not to put a stumbling block in front of any of his little ones.

The Lord is King!

So, what should our response be to *His Dark Materials* and similar books and movies? Should we be worried? Should we wring our hands in fear and desperation? Should we take to the airwaves and work to discredit Phillip Pullman and the *Northern Lights* deception?

I am troubled by this attack on God, but I remember that it's not the first time and that God, in his time, will deal with it. He is able. I'll continue to give my opinion when asked, but for the most part I won't waste more energy on the subject.

The reality is, truth always overcomes in the midst of a lie. Light always overtakes the darkness. The Word of God will be shining bright and true long after the world has forgotten about *His Dark Materials* and other schemes of Satan. Time and again throughout history, writers have worked to overthrow the authority and authenticity of Scripture. Countless people have tried to discredit the gospel of Christ. But it has never worked. They have all failed. The purveyors of evil and confusion continue to die and be buried. But Jesus is still alive, and someday every knee will bow to him!

Soon Satan and all he stands for will burn in a fiery pit. And his lies will burn there with him. But the Lord our God will still be King of kings and Lord of lords!

'No Light of Dawn'

There's a bigger issue to consider than just a book series or one family's involvement in the occult. There's a principle that goes to the heart of who the devil is and how we are to combat him. You see, the prince of darkness's greatest tactic in his war against God and all that is good is his ability to keep people from recognising the face of evil. If he can deceive, sliding under the door unnoticed, he can get access to our hearts and minds and wreak havoc in our lives. In fact, one of his greatest tricks is convincing the world that he doesn't exist.

He is a master of deceit, because deceit is all he has. Scripture calls him a liar and the father of lies.[4] The enemy has no truth; truth belongs to God and God alone. He has no power other than what God allows him to have. He has nothing to offer, nothing to promise that he can deliver on. He wins only through twisting the truth, bending God's words, clouding our eyes to reality, manipulating, deceiving, convoluting and confusing the facts.

Paul wrote, 'The god of this age has blinded the minds of unbelievers, so that they cannot see the light of the gospel of the glory of Christ.'[5] The enemy's only hope of keeping people from truth is to 'blind' them to the light of God's Word. And through this deception he has succeeded in making atheism, witchcraft and other God-dishonouring beliefs and behaviours seem harmless.

But they are not harmless. These beliefs and behaviours are gateways to the demonic. They are the devil's dark materials to lure us away from God.

God said through the prophet Isaiah, 'When men tell you to consult mediums and spiritists, who whisper and mutter, should not a people enquire of their God? Why consult the dead on behalf of the living? To the law and to the testimony! If they do not speak according to this word, they have no light of dawn.'[6]

Could it be any clearer? People who profess God as their Lord and Saviour have no business playing with sorcery or any other ungodly activity. Anyone who tries to convince you otherwise is distorting and twisting the truth. Their words have no light of dawn.

I wish my father could have experienced the joy and contentment I've felt in my life. I believed the Bible and trusted God, but Papa had no protection. I desired and discovered peace, but Papa lived nearly his entire life with no peace.

Philippians 4:7 tells us that 'the peace of God, which transcends all understanding, will guard your hearts and your minds in Christ Jesus'. What a powerful promise of comfort and protection! And it can be fulfilled in our lives as we see through the devil's deceptions and refuse to dabble in those activities that give him a hold over us.

CHAPTER 5

Trapped

The way Satan tries to keep us from grace

In a world where just about everybody is participating in social media, people seem to be lonelier than ever. In a world filled with possibilities, so many are wandering around in life, looking for purpose. With pleasure of all kinds available for the taking, men and women everywhere are empty of joy.

The devil loves it.

He is not only trying to drag people to hell with him after they die, he is also desperate to make life on earth a living hell for them. He tries to trap them in pain and suffering of all kinds and then convince them that there is no way out. I'm sure you know people who feel that way. Maybe you feel that way yourself.

The trap might be poor health. It might be an unhappy marriage. It might be an addiction. But what if there is One who can open the jaws of the trap and loose the captive? There is. God, through his Son, offers freedom to all who will follow him.

Will everybody escape their trap through Christ? Some will. Sadly, some won't.

But the point is, it *is* possible. When the devil says, 'You're trapped,' that's just another one of his lies.

Two Sides of the Wall

During my youth, when I was running wild in the streets of New York as a member of the Mau Mau gang, I lived in a small room in an upper floor of a dingy flophouse. The room consisted of nothing more than a bed, a small table and a tiny bathroom. It was a hopeless place to live, and I despised going there, because it always reminded me of how miserable my life had become.

In the apartment next to mine lived an older Jewish woman – a woman I seldom spoke a word to. Perhaps in her early eighties at that time, Mary lived alone. I often wondered why she didn't find a better neighbourhood, one that wasn't riddled with gangs and crime and people looking to do her harm. I could only imagine that this room was all she could afford, otherwise she would never have lived there. I know she was afraid of me. After all, I made sure of it, casting threatening looks at her whenever I saw her.

Each night, about three or four in the morning, I would hear Mary moaning and crying, sometimes screaming at the top of her lungs. These were the sounds of a pain whose source I did not understand. Yet I would curse at her. I would bang on the wall with my fist, telling her to shut up so I could get some sleep. Usually her cries would stop, but only for a time. Just as I was about to nod off again, the wailing would return. So I'd scream and curse even louder.

I didn't recognise it at the time, but later I would see the symmetry of the situation. There was only a wall separating us. On the one side, an old Jewish woman; on the other, a Puerto Rican teenager. We both felt trapped by a force we couldn't control. The devil had got at us, and we were lonely and tormented – just the way the devil liked it. I let my pain out through violence by day; Mary let hers out in middle-of-the-night crying. Neither one of us knew how, or if ever, we could get out of our trap.

'I Did it'

One day Mary wasn't home and I broke into her apartment to see what I could steal. Part of me wanted to get back at her for keeping me awake at night. Another part was simply driven to steal and cheat at every opportunity.

I found a handful of money wrapped in a handkerchief under her mattress – $285, not a bad haul. That was everything of value in the apartment. But I didn't hurry away. I was very cocky and self-assured in those days. So I made myself a snack in her kitchen and looked around while I ate.

There on the kitchen wall was a badly faded family photograph, the only one I had seen in the apartment. It was probably thirty years old, dating to before World War II. It showed Mary as a younger woman standing alongside what must have been her husband and two children, a boy and a girl. The boy looked a bit like me, I noticed.

Then I put it all together. The missing family members. The numbers I'd once glimpsed tattooed on her arm. The night-time crying.

This woman had survived the Holocaust.

Her family had not.

Did this revelation move me? At the time, not a bit. I finished my snack, pocketed the money, and returned to my own apartment.

Later that day, I stepped into the hallway when the police came to her apartment to investigate the crime. I stood smugly by, watching as she described the break-in and how much had been taken, watching as the officers took notes.

Mary had probably assumed that it was I who had broken into her apartment. But to make sure she knew, I waited until she was looking in my direction (and the police officers were not), and then I pointed towards myself, mouthing the words, 'I did it.' Remember: cocky and self-assured.

Mary's eyes staring back at me were cold and lifeless. Yet even though she now knew beyond doubt that I was the one who had broken into her apartment, she didn't say a word about it. She finished telling the police officers what had happened and then showed them to the door.

As they left, a strange feeling came over me. I could feel the sweat forming on my brow. *Why didn't she tell them? Why did she keep it a secret?* All she had to do was point her finger and they would have taken me away.

But she didn't. She never said a word. Never brought it up again.

Our relationship went back to what it had been. My threatening looks at her in the daytime. Her moaning and crying in the night.

The Reason Comes Out

About a year later, after God saved me from my hopeless life on the streets, and after I moved to Bible school in California to become an evangelist, I decided to go back and see Mary again. The whole time I was gone, I had never forgotten about her. In fact, I think it was when I was away at school that I began to love my neighbour. I wanted to give her back the money I had stolen and to tell her how sorry I was for taking it.

During a visit to New York, I made my way up the long, grimy stairwell to her apartment and knocked on the door. She didn't answer. So I knocked louder, making the door-frame rattle. Finally a voice from inside called out. 'Go away. Leave me alone.'

'It's me, Nicky Cruz,' I said. 'I used to be your neighbour. I just want to talk to you.'

'I know who you are,' Mary answered. 'But I don't want to talk. Go away and leave me alone.'

'I'm not here to hurt you. I just want to talk. Please let me in. I have something to give you.'

The old woman ignored my pleas, but I persisted. Eventually she saw that I wasn't going to leave, so she began unbolting the door. She must have had six or seven bolted locks, because it took her an eternity to get the door open.

'Thank you for letting me in,' I said as she stepped away from the door and stood at a safe distance. 'I came to give you something,' I said, holding out a handful of cash. It was $285, exactly the amount I had taken from her earlier.

She refused to take it. 'I don't want your money,' she said.

'Please take it,' I said. 'It's yours.'

She seemed confused by my actions. 'Why are you doing this?'

'Because I feel bad about taking your money, and I want to make it right. I'm a Christian now, and Jesus would want me to give you your money back. Please take it.' Again I held it out in her direction, with my palms open. I finally grabbed her hand and placed the money in it.

For several moments we stood in awkward silence. At last I said, 'Do you mind if I ask you something?'

She nodded for me to continue.

'The day I stole the money from your apartment, you knew I was the one who had taken it. But you didn't say anything to the police. Why didn't you tell them?'

As I had thought about it over the past year, I'd wondered if maybe she had refused to rat me out because I reminded her of her lost boy. Or maybe simply because she was afraid of my revenge. But I never dreamed of the answer she actually gave to my question.

Mary glanced at the ground, then gradually lifted her eyes to meet mine. A tear formed in the corner of her eye. 'Because you were the only person nearby I knew,' she said. 'And I knew that if anything ever happened to me, you were the only one I could count on for help and protection.'

A well of emotion burst within my spirit. I felt so ashamed about the way I had treated her. As I stood staring into her sad eyes, I wished with everything inside me that I could go back and live those years again. I wished that I could take back the hateful words I had said to her, the mean looks, the coldness.

But I couldn't. The past was over. All I could do was to try to be her friend from then on.

A Message of Freedom

The enemy has been so effective at keeping people in bondage. He has succeeded in convincing most of the world's population that we are all alone on this planet, that no one cares, that we have no one to turn to in times of need. He infuses our minds with guilt and shame and remorse. He whispers thoughts of loneliness and abandonment into the depths of our spirit. He keeps us isolated and angry and detached from those around us – like Mary and me, separated by a wall.

Satan has no heart; he wants each of us to die alone. He tells us that God doesn't care, that God is distant, that he is nowhere to be found when we need him most.

It is the coldest, darkest lie in the universe, yet people buy into it every day, just as I had once done. But the message of the cross changed everything for me. It not only set me free; it also gave me a renewed reason to live. Something greater to live for. Something beyond myself to trust in. It opened my heart to the truth that God is the Father and provider for the fatherless and the homeless. It gave me a new sense of purpose and direction and joy.

And that message is a universal one. It is the one message that every lonely soul on the planet needs to hear. The day that Jesus hung on the cross, with a crown of thorns digging into his brow and blood trickling from the nail holes in his hands and feet, he offered hope in the face of hopelessness. He saw what I saw that day when I stood in the doorway of a dingy apartment, staring into the lonely eyes of my ex-neighbour.

He saw the face of an angry and lost nineteen-year-old running the streets of New York, scratching and clawing for survival, looking for hope in the midst of a dangerous street gang.

He saw the face of my parents as they struggled each day to find meaning and significance within the world of the occult.

He saw the face of every lost and lonely soul on the planet, and it brought untold pain to his spirit. The outward scars he suffered were nothing compared to the ones that pierced his heart.

These are the faces that led him to the cross. These are the ones he died for. These are the lost sheep he came to earth to find.

And on the cross, he found them. The blood of Jesus brought hope to the hopeless, now and forevermore!

Just a Number?

After Gloria and I married and came to New York to live, I couldn't wait to introduce my bride to my old neighbour. As soon as I could, I took Gloria to Mary's apartment and knocked several times. But there was only silence. So I went to the nearby dry-cleaners, where the people had known both Mary and me, and asked about her.

They told me she had passed away.

I was so sad when I found out she had died alone and had been buried in an unmarked grave. The only identification was a number. Mary was buried with a number, like the number that had identified her years before in the concentration camp.

I don't know if she ever turned to her Messiah in faith. I don't know if she ever escaped the trap the devil had placed her in. But for those of us who are still living and breathing, we can be released from our traps through Jesus. And when that happens, it will be a powerful blow against Satan in the cosmic spiritual war.

CHAPTER 6

Terror in the Night

The threat of personal attack

When I was a child, Satan constantly messed with my mind. He would endlessly taunt me. I had nightmares almost every night – horrible images that I can still see in my mind when I close my eyes.

Even after I moved to New York and was away from my mom and dad, and joined a gang, the attacks continued. The nightmares wouldn't go away. And some of my most frightening and intense experiences with the world of evil came *after* I had given my heart to Jesus, not before. I was sure they would stop once I surrendered to Jesus, but for a while they actually grew worse.

Now, let me say up front that I don't believe that Christians can be possessed by demons. In all my years of ministering around the world, I have never seen that happen. Christians can, however, be *oppressed* by evil spirits. I'll be saying more about this distinction in Chapter 10. Right now, I just want to make the very important point that, as Christ's followers, we need to expect attacks of many kinds from our enemies in the spiritual realm.

The first time this happened to me as a Christian was just three weeks after my conversion.

An Unlikely Setting for Demonic Attack

When I became a believer, David Wilkerson knew that I needed to get out of New York in order to be protected from the gangs. I had been a warlord for the notorious Mau Mau gang in New York, and news of my new-found faith in Jesus spread quickly to other gangs in the area, making me a target. The only way I could survive would be to get away until things settled down. So Wilkerson introduced me to a family who agreed to take me in.

I knew them only as Mr and Mrs Hostrander, and I couldn't even say their name properly, since I spoke very little English at the time. The Hostranders lived in a middle-class neighbourhood of Williamsburg, Pennsylvania. They had two kids of their own and often took in foster kids or strays from the street. I could barely communicate with them, but I didn't have to. They were so good to me, so kind and loving. This was a long way from the lonely apartment I had occupied on the other side of the wall from Mary!

I had spent my entire childhood in rebellion, always looking for trouble, but now I was determined to change all that. I was serious about my new walk with the Lord and I wanted a new life. I felt different inside, clean and pure and innocent, and I wanted to show that to others by being kind – something I knew little about. So I obeyed the Hostranders, no matter what they asked me to do. All my life I'd acted like a little devil, but now I was a little angel.

Each night the Hostranders went to bed extremely early, sometimes as early as 6.30 or 7pm. I was used to staying up well past midnight, hanging out with my gang or looking for trouble in the streets. Some days I didn't even get up until 7 in the evening. But now all that had changed. I was determined to go to bed the same time as the Hostranders. I'm not even sure they expected me to, but I wanted to please them, whatever that took.

Most nights I would lie in bed watching the sun go down from my bedroom window on the top floor of their house. I couldn't sleep, but I didn't care. I spent the time praying or reading the new Bible that David Wilkerson had given me. But most of the time I would lie in bed praising God, thanking him for saving me. I would thank him for the Hostranders, for the comfortable bed they let me sleep in and for the beautiful view out the window of my new bedroom. So much in my life had changed, thanks to Jesus.

But at least one thing hadn't changed. The demons that haunted me as a child still longed to hurt me, just as they had done so many nights during my childhood. Only now they were really angry. They were furious at me for giving my heart and my life to Jesus.

David had sent me to Pennsylvania to hide me from the New York gangs. But there was no place where he could hide me from my enemies in the spirit realm.

The Weight of Evil

One night I was lying in bed, gazing out the closed window, thinking of nothing in particular, when suddenly the curtain began to move. It happened in an instant and, based on my past experiences, I instinctively feared it might be an evil spirit. Then, before I could say a word, an invisible entity pounced on top of my body, constricting my throat and pushing me down onto the bed. The weight was greater than anything I had ever experienced as a young boy, as if this time Satan himself had come to torment me. I tried to speak, to call out to the Hostranders for help, but nothing came out of my mouth. I couldn't even breathe. It was a horribly helpless feeling – a powerlessness that couldn't possibly be described in words. All the while I heard strange noises, whispering and screeching inside my head, noises that couldn't be deciphered as words but were clearly meant to frighten me. Unintelligible, demonic voices.

I thought this unseen spirit would kill me. No matter how hard I struggled, I couldn't break free, couldn't move, couldn't speak or breathe or even grunt.

Suddenly I remembered something David Wilkerson had told me just a few weeks earlier, during one of our first Bible studies together after I became a Christian. He said that if evil spirits ever came near, I was to call on the blood of Jesus. He said that demons have no power over the blood of Jesus, and they have to flee in its presence. Even the name of Jesus burns their ears and sends them running for cover. So I started calling on Jesus. Though I couldn't speak, I said in my mind, over and over, 'The blood of Jesus! The blood of Jesus! The blood of Jesus!'

The demon wouldn't stop right away. But I kept repeating the phrase in my thoughts, knowing that Jesus would save me. Suddenly I was able to open my mouth, and the words burst out, much louder than I expected them to: 'The blood of Jesus, save me!'

At that instant the spirit lifted from my body and let go of my throat. I could feel him leaping away from me, almost as if he had been grabbed and thrown. I lifted my head just in time to see the curtains in front of the window fly open as the evil, unseen spirit bolted out of the room. My heart was racing a thousand miles an hour, and I kept crying over and over, 'Thank you, Jesus! Thank you for saving me! Thank you!'

The Meaning of the Attack

It was a long time before I could stop shaking, and sweat was pouring down the sides of my face. I had been through a horrible experience. And as thankful as I was that Christ had rescued me, I was confused by what had happened. Sitting on the edge of my bed, I wondered, *Why would God allow this to happen? How can evil still taunt me now that I've given my life to Jesus?*

Today I have a better understanding of the dynamics of what was going on that night. I now realise how critical this event was to my future. It was Satan's last great attempt to steal my soul back from God. I had been baptised the day before this happened, and the devil was determined to try and destroy my new-found faith.

The devil had tried to plant fear in me from my childhood. After my conversion, I was just a baby Christian and I didn't know Scripture. I didn't know much of anything about the faith. So the enemy used this opportunity to attempt to instil fear in me again. It was a strategic move on his part, but it failed to accomplish the goal.

It was one of the most frightening moments of my life. The enemy was battling for my soul, and had he won that battle I might have fallen back into his hands. But I remained firm. I knew I had to overcome the spirits that haunted me as a child and I was resolved to do just that. I'm convinced that determination secured my future forever.

And more than that, what the devil meant for harm, God turned to good. I think of that day as the beginning of my understanding about the devil. The knowledge I have today, and the intimacy I have with my Lord, tells me that the evil one cannot harm me.[1] The truth is, he is subject to the authority of Christ – an authority lent to believers like me. And as we grow up in Christ, we learn that we are no longer hostages to the enemy. We have weapons at our disposal.

When I called on the blood of Jesus that night, Satan's demon fled in fear.[2] had no choice but to run. As a child, I had been helpless against the demons' taunting, but now I knew they could never again hold power over my life. I was covered by the blood of Jesus, and my soul remains secure in his loving arms!

The Power to Overcome Evil

My experience that night was a turning point for me. But what is my point in telling it to you? Just this: you will be attacked by Satan and his rebellious spirits. I hope it won't be as direct and scary as what happened to me that night in the Hostranders' home. But it will happen.

Maybe you'll be afflicted with some kind of mental or physical ailment. Maybe you'll encounter strange and disturbing manifestations designed to frighten you. Maybe you'll have to fight against trends in society that are satanically inspired. Often you'll be tempted to sin and abandon the path of holiness God has called you to. We'll be learning more about such schemes of the devil in future chapters. But regardless what form it takes, you *will* be attacked.

And I have some more bad news for you. When these attacks come, you won't be able to resist them. Not in your own strength, that is. Your personal willpower is just not enough. Remember, Lucifer was created as the greatest of the angels before he revolted against God. We are foolish to minimise his power or exaggerate our own.

In the book of Jude, the writer set out to speak of the salvation that believers share in Christ. But around the eighth verse his words take a strange detour. The Holy Spirit directed him to include a warning to believers who might discount the powers of darkness. Referring to certain sinners, he wrote, 'These dreamers pollute their own bodies, reject authority and slander celestial beings. But even the archangel Michael, when he was disputing with the devil about the body of Moses, did not dare to bring a slanderous accusation against him, but said, "The Lord rebuke you!"[3]

It's an interesting passage that seems mysteriously vague and out of place. And Jude doesn't elaborate any further. Yet he gives us a clear warning against 'slandering' Satan, or taking spiritual warfare into our own hands. When it comes to the supernatural world, we are to let God deal with Satan and his demons. Our job is to call on the blood of Jesus and allow his grace to shield and protect us from harm.

We're not strong enough on our own to defeat the attacks of evil spirits. But the point is, we're *not* on our own. If you are a believer, then, just like me, you are covered by the blood of Jesus. His blood saves us in the first place and it continues to protect us throughout our lives on this earth.

The blood of Jesus represents God's power and authority. He has chosen to redeem and preserve a people for himself through the sacrifice of Christ on the cross. That blood is like a cloak of protection that the devil and his demons can never penetrate when we wear it.

We must never forget, never stray away from, the cross of Jesus and his blood. His blood is the power we need.

The Miracle of Jesus' Blood

Picture the hill of Calvary on that great and terrible day when the Lord was taken there.

The cross in the centre seems to tower over the onlookers. The sky is as dark as if Lucifer's own mighty wing were obscuring the sun. And there, struggling for breath to continue living just a little longer, hangs the sinless Son of God.

Blood drips from his forehead, where a circle of thorns was cruelly forced onto his head. More blood drips from his wrists and ankles, because of the crude iron spikes that were driven through flesh and bone. Before all is done, blood mixed with water will gush from his side as a soldier drives in a spear to guarantee his death.

And drop by drop, this blood drips down. It drips down his precious body, drips down that cross made of wood, drips all the way to the ground. It ennobles the earth where it falls. And we can even say that it spreads throughout the world today, wherever men and women turn to Christ in faith for salvation.

The blood that coursed through the veins of Jesus as he walked the earth was the only blood in all of history powerful enough to seal God's forgiveness once and for all. It was the only blood whole enough to forever bridge the gap between God and humanity, the only blood pure enough to whiten any heart that cries out to God for salvation.

Only the blood of Jesus could seal the fate of Satan once and for all. Through the shedding of Christ's blood on the cross, Satan suffered the ultimate defeat. Through the cross, God's wrath was appeased. And through the cross, through the power of Jesus' blood, you and I can find complete victory over sin and darkness and death.

The book of Revelation refers to believers who 'overcame [the devil] by the blood of the Lamb and by the word of their testimony'.[4] So, as you look ahead to the possibility of evil entities attacking you, as one attacked me years ago in a small town in Pennsylvania, I can give you no better advice than the simple words David Wilkerson used with me. Call out, 'The blood of Jesus! The blood of Jesus!' That blood is a protective covering to you, but it is a poison to the demons. Rely on the power of God in the blood of Jesus, and the demons will flee and you will be safe.

CHAPTER 7

The Devil in Disguise

He's not what he seems

Often, the devil's strategy is to hide his true nature of wickedness. At times, in fact, he might come across as downright appealing. He's likeable. Or at least, he has some kind of strange attraction. What's happening here? As the apostle Paul explained, the devil sometimes 'masquerades as an angel of light'.[1] Formerly a beautiful and God-honouring angel, Lucifer can still act the part when it is to his advantage. In short, he is a master of disguise, frequently taking on the form of good in order to deceive.

That's why so many religions and cults use terms that sound almost Christian, yet their meaning is entirely different. The devil deceives by mixing a little truth with his lies.

That's why witchcraft and sorcery and other occult practices have spread so far and wide. At first they seem intriguing and different, so people dabble in them to see what happens. But that's all it takes to bring down your defences and draw you in.

And that's why sin is so deadly in our lives. It always seems like such a little thing. Just a white lie, a 'harmless' glance at pornography, a quick experimentation with drugs. Then another lie, another glance, another taste. And before we know it, we are naked in our soul and defenceless. And that's when the enemy pounces.

It's said that snakes sometimes 'paralyse' their prey with their glittering, reflective eyes, holding them in place with a kind of fascination until the snake can strike. Satan does the same to Christians who are vulnerable. He catches our interest. We don't immediately see his true awfulness; instead we are drawn in and want to see more.

Sooner or later, though, it becomes clear – painfully clear – what the devil is really like. However much he may look like an angel of light, he's still the prince of darkness. The serpent is poised to strike.

Mentored by Satan

Our office once received a letter from a man named Danny. He wrote that he had grown up in a good household, with attentive and loving parents, yet something within him seemed drawn towards evil. It was a fascination he didn't understand or want, yet it somehow compelled him.

Danny wrote of one of his earliest memories. He was eight years old, and walking up the stairs to his bedroom, when suddenly he sensed an evil presence. A dark spirit engulfed him, rushing through his entire body, causing him to think horrible thoughts. It was a strange sensation, something he'd never expected, clearly demonic.

Through the years this evil spirit visited Danny on a regular basis, always beckoning him to do things he knew he shouldn't do. He said it felt as if he were being mentored by Satan himself.

At the age of ten, Danny found a vacant building and began going there regularly to play. The spirits would always be there with him, encouraging him to do evil things. He built an altar to Satan and began burning candles and incense, even set Bibles on fire. He had no idea why he did these things, only that the compulsion towards evil was too powerful to resist.

One day the police searched the building and found the makeshift altar. They discovered who had built it and confronted Danny in front of his parents. They were convinced that he had joined a satanic coven in a nearby neighbourhood, since the rituals he performed by himself were identical to the ceremonies that the Satanists performed during their services. Yet Danny had no idea what a satanic coven was. He was simply doing what the evil spirits taught him.

Danny's letter goes on to describe his childhood of crime and violence and hate, which eventually led to prison. His apprenticeship in evil bore its expected fruit.

Network of Evil

Danny's story is unusual in at least one respect. Normally, people who are heavily influenced by demons get that way because they have been exposed to evil influences, such as happened to me through the spiritism that was practised at my childhood home. Danny, though, seems to have been mentored directly by demons in how to be a Satanist.

But in another way, Danny's story is all too typical. It began with his becoming fascinated with the devil and devilish practices. He did not fully realise what he was getting into . . . until he was already deep inside the devil's web of deception. This is a story that's been retold again and again.

Let me point out one means that the devil, with seeming innocence, uses to work his way into many lives today. It's a means that is particularly insidious for our children and youth. From the stories I've told, you may have noticed already that the devil often attacks the young, just as he did me in Puerto Rico and just as he did Danny. Sadly, in the rest of this book, I will have still more stories to tell about demonic attacks on children. The devil has no mercy towards the young and innocent. Remember, he is motherless – a hardened, hopeless case. And one particular means he is using to great effect against our children and grandchildren today is technology.

Think about the Internet for a moment. Of course it's an incredibly powerful and useful tool. But at the same time it has beguiling, hidden, pervasive qualities. What could be more tailor-made for the devil's use? It's a perfect tool for invisible deception and temptation. Through the Internet's words, images and sounds, the devil can get at people all around the world in utter stealth. The Internet thus is a source of untold danger and temptation for its users, especially teenagers, who use it the most.

Pornography is so accessible online that kids find themselves bombarded by sexual images. Teenagers have become so accustomed to seeing lurid images that they don't even recognise it as harmful. Many young girls take provocative pictures of themselves and post them on the Internet. Often these images are texted or e-mailed to friends, only to spread like wildfire through teenage social networks. When an anonymous video chatting website went online, exhibitionists around the world quickly seized on it as the perfect way to expose their bodies to others, including children.

One police officer told of raiding the home of a suspected child molester, only to find several notebooks filled with meticulous information about dozens of children – their pictures, where they lived, what they liked to do, what their schedules were. Where did he get this information? From Facebook. All the information had been voluntarily posted there by the children themselves or their parents. I shudder to think what the predator would have done with the information if he'd had more time.

Yet the worst happens all the time, and sexual deviancy on the supposedly innocent Internet is almost always involved. A child leaves home on a bicycle . . . and is never heard from again. A girl walks to a friend's house . . . and is found days later in a ditch. College girls think they are safe walking on their own campus . . . and then they are pulled into the shadows and attacked. It's horrible to contemplate what goes on. (I am so angry as I write this chapter!)

A man I know with a large Christian organisation was warped by Internet porn, like so many others. He was caught using online chat to try to lure a young teenager into a situation where he could take advantage of her. In the aftermath of this disclosure, he asked me to counsel him! Frankly, what he needed wasn't counsel but confession – and some jail time.

Dear Lord, what is wrong with our society? I'm tired of seeing the pain and grief on the faces of parents who are trying to deal with these kinds of things. And I haven't even gotten to the other ways that the evil side can use the Internet to create havoc and destruction among our youth. Online gambling. Cyber bullying. Identity theft. Exposure to violent images, racist messages and perversion. Depression and social isolation. Addiction to the Internet itself. It's happening all the time, in homes throughout my neighbourhood and yours.

If you are a parent, I urge you to instil good Internet practices in your children's lives. Use web-filtering software, limit Internet usage and closely monitor and talk about what your children are doing online. Such precautions may not remove all threats, but they will go a long way towards protecting your children. It's far better than doing nothing.

The prophet Isaiah warned, 'Woe to those who call evil good and good evil, who put darkness for light and light for darkness, who put bitter for sweet and sweet for bitter.'[2] His words should serve as a stern rebuke of those who take evil too lightly. As I've said before, the beast is loose and he is at war with the youth of the world like never before.

I'm thankful to be able to say that Danny – the young man who wrote me about worshipping Satan as a child – finally found freedom from his life of evil. A guard at his prison led him to Christ and today he is a new person. He went back to school, even got a Bible degree, and is living his life for Jesus.

That is wonderful news! Sadly, though, not all who are deceived by the 'angel of light' escape his clutches. And even when some do, it can be tremendously difficult. That's the way it was for my father.

A Lie from Hell

I'll never forget the day in 1964 when I got a call from my mother informing me that Papa was sick and in the hospital. After struggling for years with heart problems, he had suffered a massive heart attack and the doctors were afraid he wouldn't live through the night. As soon as I could, I caught a plane from New York to Puerto Rico.

I was thrilled to see that Papa was still alive when I reached him. I stood over his bed and said to him, 'Don Galo, you need to make things right with Jesus. You are lost and only God can save you. The god you follow has destroyed our family. He has brought untold pain to you and Mama and the rest of our household. I want you to go to heaven with me. Why don't you give your heart to Jesus?'

He looked at me with his sad and longing eyes. 'I can't, son,' he said. 'I'm scared.'

I was completely taken aback by this. For two reasons. It was the first time I had ever heard him call me 'son', and because of this, I could hardly contain my tears. It was also the first time I'd ever heard Papa say he was frightened. I didn't think Papa was afraid of anything.

'You don't know what I've done,' he continued. 'You don't

know the horrible things I've brought upon our family. After all the pacts I've made with witchcraft, if I turn my back on the spirits, they will condemn me forever. Satan will be so upset that he will kill you all. You don't know what they're capable of. You don't know how they haunt me. I can't betray the spirits. I can't do that to my family!'

'That is a lie from hell!' I told him. 'I want to tell you, and I want you to take this into your heart of hearts: Satan can't touch your wife and he can't touch me or Frank or Chelo or Ralphie. Don't believe those lies. The spirits can't harm us. We're covered by the blood of Jesus. The Spirit of God is here, and he is far more powerful than any evil spirit. The only one who is going to be hurt today is Satan! Jesus has defeated him. We are God's property, so you have nothing to fear. Renounce your religion and accept Jesus as your Saviour!'

Papa's eyes grew wide with fright. 'Don't say that,' he said. 'Don't make the spirits angry!'

I could see in his eyes that he longed to believe me, but something inside him resisted. He couldn't get past his fears. He was still a slave to the enemy's deceptions. Nothing I could say would convince him to think differently.

I left his side that day knowing that he still had not accepted Jesus as his Saviour. Silently I prayed, 'Lord, don't let Papa die tonight. Keep him alive until we can get through to him. Help him overcome his fears and doubts. Help him accept the truth about his evil religion and turn away from it. Give us the strength and time to reach Papa before he faces eternity.'

A Change of Heart

After our visit in the hospital, Papa went home, expecting to die soon. In fact, though, he lived on for another year. I continued to pray for him. So did the others in my family who had become Christians, especially my mother, who had received Christ and renounced spiritism four years earlier.

Then, one day, during another trip home, I took a Christian businessman named Choco to see my father. Choco was a highly respected man in our region and Papa held him in the highest regard. I asked Choco to pray for my father, hoping he would be able to get through to him.

At the time my father had a dog named Tuti and we were all convinced that the dog was demon possessed. I know this sounds strange, but if you lived with us, you would understand why we thought this. He always stayed close to Papa and would do strange things whenever Papa would summon the spirits. Tuti was simply not normal; that's the only way I know to describe it.

When Choco came to pray for my father – the minute he began to speak – Tuti started convulsing and acting strange. When Choco said the name 'Jesus', Tuti leaped towards his throat, trying to bite him on the neck. Choco instinctively brought his hand in front of his face and knocked the little dog across the room. Tuti must have hit his head, because he lay unconscious on the floor. My father laughed at the scene, then listened carefully as Choco prayed for him. Afterwards Papa fell into a deep and restful sleep – the first sleep he had gotten in several days.

At times we wondered if he would ever wake up. He lay completely still. He was still breathing, so we knew he was alive; he just couldn't wake up. Like he was in some kind of a strange coma or trance.

While he was still in his coma, I left Puerto Rico to go home. I heard from my mother what happened next.

After days of sleeping, my father suddenly woke up. He began calling for my mother, saying, 'Aleja, Aleja, Aleja, Aleja.' Four times he called her name and she ran to him. He had tears running down his face and he said, 'I'm ready to give my life to Jesus! Pray for me, Aleja. I surrender! I renounce the spirits! I renounce my religion! I want Jesus to save me!'

My mother prayed with my father, asking Jesus to come into his heart and make him a new person. They cried together as Papa accepted Jesus as his Lord and Saviour. My father knew in his heart he had been forgiven and he knew my mother was in good hands. He was now ready to go.

About eight hours later Papa died, still praising God with his lips. The last words out of his mouth were words of thanksgiving to his new Saviour.

One of the biggest regrets of my life is that I was not there to witness my father's salvation. But every time I think of it, I have to smile. I can just imagine how frustrated the devil was at that moment. Jesus snatched my father from the threshold of hell and escorted him straight to heaven by his holy angels. I have no doubt there was extreme anger in hell that day!

The Devil as He Really is

Today I know that both Papa and Mama are waiting for me in heaven and someday we'll have a glorious reunion. My only regret is that Satan was able to hold them both hostage to his lies for so many years during their days on earth. He didn't succeed in dragging them into the pit of hell with him, but he did succeed in making much of their lives on earth miserable. For that I despise him even more deeply.

My parents never imagined that they were serving Satan. They didn't claim to be worshipping evil or giving credence to the devil. They called their practices 'white magic' and focused on summoning 'good spirits', not evil ones. They didn't understand what they were doing, only that the power they were able to summon was genuine and enticing and addictive.

But the spirits they brought were not good. And the doorway to hell they opened brought unspeakable terror into our home. Their falling for the devil's masquerade was very costly indeed.

If only every soul immersed in sin and rebellion could see what I've seen. If only I could show every witch and warlock and sorcerer just a glimpse of the eternal fate that awaits them unless they turn away from their evil practices. If only through Jesus I could free every heart held captive by Satan's lies.

I'm certain that no one would ever willingly follow Satan if they saw him for what he truly is – a deceiving, hateful, vengeful demon from hell! When people truly see this, they want nothing to do with the devil, because no one willingly gives their life over to a loser. The devil promises power, but eventually Satan has power over you, a bondage that is like no other.

We have to rip off the devil's mask. We have to recognise the darkness behind the light. We have to see the devil for the hideous deceiver he really is. God will help us to do this and will keep us safe from our enemy, for God is truly all light!

CHAPTER 8

In the Crosshairs

How our enemy seeks to hurt us

Guatemala, 1970: ten-year-old Hector recovered from his brief unconsciousness and opened his eyes. He was lying in the street. A short distance away was his family's BMW, twisted around a pole, fumes and liquid spewing from beneath the warped hood. He saw his sister, bleeding, lying in the arms of a paramedic. He saw his aunt in the back of the car, her head propped against the far window. He saw strangers running back and forth, some purposeful, others simply confused or curious.

Hector remembered the sound of gunshots coming from the back seat. Then nothing more until he woke up on the street.

Before the shooting and the accident, he had been sitting in the front seat with his little sister on his lap. So, how had he ended up here on the street? And in all that violence, why was he completely unharmed?

It was the lowest – and most confusing – moment of a life more terrible than any child should have to experience.

A Chaotic Life

Hector Nufio was born in 1960 in the city of Antigua, Guatemala. But the roots of his life of misery reached back even further.

His mother's name was Dolores, which means 'pain' in Spanish. She was given that name as a baby because her own mother died giving birth to her. It appeared to be a prophetic act, because the years to follow were riddled with heartache and disappointment. Dolores had a difficult youth, then as an adult married a man who made his money at shady business deals. The two spent much of their time running from people who wanted them dead.

Hector was born into a family in chaos, and his mother feared for his life. So when he was three she gave him to his aunt and uncle in order to keep him safe. A few years later, Hector's mother had another child, this one a girl named Mari Flor. She, too, was given to her aunt and uncle to raise in order to keep her safe. The mother's fears were not unfounded. Just a few months later, the children's father was shot dead in the street by a sniper on top of a nearby building. Dolores feared that she was the next target.

So Hector and Mari Flor spent their childhood in the care of their aunt and uncle – people they would eventually embrace as their parents. On the surface this seemed to be a happy family. The couple ran several businesses and had all the conveniences of wealth, including a nice house, expensive furniture, designer clothes and even a BMW in the garage. But that was just how things looked on the

76

outside. The family was anything but happy. Hector's aunt was cold and angry towards the children and their uncle seemed filled with secrets of his own.

Hector spent countless nights alone in his room, in fear of his aunt and uncle, and with few friends to turn to for consolation. He was physically and emotionally abused by his aunt. The rejection he felt drove him to become deeply shy and introverted. His biological mother was nowhere to be found and his caretakers seemed to care more about money than kids. It was a lonely existence.

A Choice

Hector was ten when his world turned upside down. That's when his aunt learned that her husband was having an affair. She was not the forgiving type. In her anger she sat Hector down at the table and said, 'Listen, your uncle and I are getting a divorce and you need to decide who you're going to go with. Are you going to stay with me, or are you going to go with your uncle?'

It was a decision no ten-year-old should ever have to make, but she was intent on getting an answer.

'I can't decide,' Hector cried. 'I love you both!' Then he ran to his room in tears.

Minutes later a shot rang out. Hector dashed back to his aunt's room, fearing the worst. She was sitting on her bed with a smoking gun in her lap, still alive but shaking with anger. 'You see what just happened?' she screamed. 'You see what I did!'

Hector noticed a bullet hole in the far wall.

'The next time, I will shoot myself if you don't go with me!' she told him. 'I swear I'll do it! Don't make me kill myself!'

It wasn't the first time her unstable personality had raised its ugly head, but for Hector it was certainly the most distressing so far. He knew he could never cross her. He could only imagine what she might be capable of doing.

The couple separated, and for several months Hector and Mari Flor lived with their aunt. It was a frightening time for the kids, because the future seemed so unpredictable. They did their best to steer clear of their aunt's rages.

Then one day their uncle showed up on the doorstep declaring that he had come back to the family. He said he wanted to reconcile with his wife and even planned to move the family to Spain in an effort to make a fresh start. The kids were elated and hurried to pack their things.

What Hector didn't know was that his uncle's return was simply an attempt to free the kids from their aunt's household. His plan was to take the children to Spain and leave his wife behind. His wife played along, but she wasn't fooled by his words. And the devil had planted a horrific idea in the mind of this disturbed woman.

'Fireworks'

When the fateful day arrived, the family loaded into their BMW to make the long trip to the Spanish Embassy. It was to be the first stop on their move to Spain. His aunt seemed particularly distant and strange that day. Instead of climbing into her regular seat beside her husband, she put Hector in the front passenger seat of the car and then placed his four-year-old sister on his lap. 'Today everything is going to end,' she said to the kids outside their uncle's hearing. 'There is going to be fireworks, then we'll have a huge party, because today everything is going to end. We're going to be one big happy family again.'

The embassy was closed when the family pulled into the parking lot, so they were forced to turn around and start the long drive back to their home. They talked about beginning their journey the next day. It was disappointing to the kids, but there wasn't much else they could do.

The car turned a corner just two blocks from their home, and Hector craned his neck to see the street over his sister's bobbing head, hoping to get a glimpse of his driveway. At that moment a deafening noise shattered the silence and shook the frame of the car. Then it came again. Then again. Shots from a gun, all coming from the back seat.

That is all Hector remembers. He has no recollection of his uncle lunging against the steering wheel, of his sister screaming in pain, of the car careening through the neighbourhood, eventually crashing into a lamppost. No memory of anything that happened. Just gunshots, then nothing.

The next memory he has is of opening his eyes and seeing the aftermath unfolding before him: the car twisted around a pole, his sister bleeding, his aunt in the back seat, strangers running back and forth. He watched the scene as if it were all playing out on a cinema screen in front of him, enthralled by the action but curiously removed from it. A ticket-holder for a show called Calamity. Nothing but a spectator.

He didn't understand what had happened, but he got up and went to his sister's side. She was crying uncontrollably, cradled in the arms of a paramedic.

'Is she OK?' Hector cried.

'We're doing all we can,' said the paramedic. 'The ambulance will be here soon. Don't worry, I'll take care of her.'

Then he looked again at his aunt in the back seat of the car, her eyes open but apparently unseeing. Blood was gushing from her head. Hector winced at the sight, cradling his head in his hands.

But where was his uncle? What had happened to him?

At that moment his aunt passed out. Hector watched helplessly as her eyes glanced at him, then slowly glazed over, rolling into the back of her head. Hector was haunted by the thought of her dying at that moment. Hector hoped that his aunt would live to speak to him once more, so he could tell her how much he loved her.

Hector sat on a nearby curb and wept as police officers worked to bring sense to the chaos. An eternity came and went as the horrific scene was systematically cleared away. The car was towed to a nearby garage, his sister taken away in an ambulance, his aunt carried away on a stretcher, the glass and debris swept from the street by a man in grey overalls, and one by one, strangers disappeared into the distance.

He slowly walked towards their home, opened the front door, and made his way upstairs to his bedroom. There he lay on his bed and wept.

Questions Answered and Unanswered

Later Hector would learn more and piece together the events of that day. In a fit of rage his aunt had shot his uncle and sister before turning the gun on herself.

Three bullets pierced his uncle's back, puncturing his lungs in the process. After the crash, his uncle made it to his feet and started walking aimlessly through the streets, looking for help. A stranger picked him up and carried him to a nearby emergency room. He was barely alive when they arrived. He died soon afterwards.

Hector's sister was shot twice in the leg. She was cared for in the hospital, where she eventually made a full recovery.

After firing the gun several times, his aunt shot herself in the head with a single bullet. The cause of all this mayhem, she died at the scene of the accident.

But what happened to me? Hector would often think. *Why wasn't I shot like my sister and uncle? I was right there in the front seat with them. There's no way the bullet could have missed me and hit my sister. And why was I not hurt from the crash? Why don't I remember anything that happened?*

Hector and his sister eventually came back into the custody of their biological mother, and she did her best to raise them on her own. But the years were uncertain and life brought lots of sorrow into their home. And Hector still struggled to understand what had happened to him.

Home

Having moved to the USA, Hector entered the military at the age of seventeen and soon afterwards married his high school sweetheart, Marylin. It was 1979, and the Iran hostage crisis was in full swing. Hector found himself on a battleship in the Mediterranean practising manoeuvres with his fellow marines. It was a dangerous mission, and many of the men were on their knees praying. Hector considered himself a good person but knew little about the kind of faith that others seemed to have.

One fellow marine, a man named Peter, started preaching to Hector. 'If you don't accept Jesus into your heart, you're going to go to hell,' the man told him. The words might have had more effect if Peter hadn't been such a hypocrite. Hector knew him as a drinker and a womaniser – a man who seldom practised what he preached. But still the man persisted. 'You're going to hell, Hector! You need to accept Jesus!'

Hector was so put off by Peter's verbal attacks that he started reading the Bible for himself, just to find a way to prove the man wrong. He began at the beginning and read the Bible all the way through, then started again. Over the next two months he read the Bible cover to cover four times through. And with each reading his heart softened a little more.

He soon realised that he was a sinner who needed forgiveness. So one day, while sitting in his bed in the belly of the ship, he lifted his eyes to heaven and asked Jesus to come into his heart. 'I've been running for so long,' he said, 'but I don't want to run anymore. I've been so angry with you for the things that have happened in our family, and I still don't understand it, but I want to trust you. Forgive me, Jesus. Come into my heart and make me whole again.'

Hector surrendered. It was a profound experience of faith and the beginning of a new life in Christ – a happiness that he had never known before.

At that instant Hector felt God speaking to his spirit. It was an undeniable voice in the core of his being. God was calling him to be a minister. Not just to give his heart to Jesus, but to give his career to God as well. It was a calling that confused Hector, since he had no idea where this would take him and his wife, but he committed to following wherever God might lead him.

After a lifetime of pain and confusion, Hector had finally come home.

From Tragedy to Testimony

That event happened more than thirty years ago, and today Hector is still walking the path of obedience. He finished his stint in the military and then threw himself into the ministry, becoming an effective and respected teacher. He pastored and founded several churches in Chicago, and then he went back to Guatemala, where he currently pastors a church of twelve thousand with multiple Sunday services. His church also has over five hundred branch churches in many different countries. God took his tragedy and turned it into a life filled with victory.

It hasn't been an easy road. His past has haunted him along the way. Hector has suffered through several bouts of depression and anxiety, but he's never turned his back on God. He has remained faithful in spite of the hardship.

For much of his life he wondered why he wasn't injured in the accident with his sister or hit by the bullets his aunt fired in his direction. Then one day he had a chance to talk with his sister about the ordeal. They were both adults, having dinner together, when his sister said to him, 'There's something I've always wanted to ask you. What happened to you that day?'

'What do you mean?' Hector responded.

'Well, I remember sitting on your lap and suddenly you disappeared. You just vanished. Then the next thing I knew, I was hit in the leg by a bullet and the car went out of control. But where did you go?'

At that instant Hector suddenly realised why he had survived. It was a miracle. He'd always known that the bullet that hit his sister was meant for him, yet he came away unscathed. God had miraculously saved his life, though he never knew why. He suddenly understood why he had no memory of the event and no injuries. Why he opened his eyes to find himself completely removed from the scene, lying in the street, several yards away.

God had saved him for a reason. And now it was clear why. Because God wanted to take the tragedy of Hector's life and turn it into a powerful testimony of faith. God wanted to redeem the pain of Hector's past and use it to create a mighty warrior for the kingdom.

The Transformation

I'm glad to be Hector Nufio's friend, and I am grateful to him for letting me use his story in this book. I tell it to you because I want you to see what the devil can do to us. And how God can redeem what the devil has tried to keep for himself.

Hector and his sister were placed in a home where evil resided. Their aunt was mentally ill. She needed clinical help, but she didn't get it. And so Satan, being so slick, entered the castle of her mind and directed her to kill her husband. She did just that.

Some people say to me, 'Aren't the devil and his demons restricted to making evil suggestions and offering deceptions? They can't afflict people directly, can they?' Sadly, yes, they can. Both mentally and physically. It's true that Satan can't ever know what we are thinking; only God can know our thoughts, intentions and motives.[1] But he works in our minds and bodies anyway.

Consider the Bible's evidence on this. An evil spirit unbalanced King Saul's mind. Evil spirits whom Jesus encountered stole people's hearing, sight and speech. They would shake their victims, throw them into fire and water and cause convulsions. One woman suffered from a bent back for years because of her evil spirit.[2] Even the apostle Paul admitted, 'There was given me a thorn in the flesh, a messenger of Satan, to torment me.'[3] This 'thorn' is presumed to be some kind of health problem, possibly failing eyesight.

The most instructive story of demonic affliction in the Bible is the story of Job. In the Bible book named after this ancient ranch owner, we see the veil pulled back on the workings of the spiritual realm. Satan came to the Lord and asked permission to test Job. With that permission granted, first he destroyed all of Job's children, servants and flocks. Then he 'afflicted Job with painful sores from the soles of his feet to the top of his head'.[4]

I believe that Satan still inflicts sickness, injury and mental illness on people from time to time. I'm not saying that every affliction can be directly or entirely attributed to evil forces. But it happens. The devil loves to use these tactics to harm and discourage his victims. And even when he's not personally responsible for human suffering, you can bet he cheers it on.

But remember something else the story of Job shows us. Satan cannot afflict anyone without God's permission, and God puts limits on what he will allow. (If God didn't apply limits, the devil would have us all writhing in agony.) Furthermore, God has important reasons for what he allows, as difficult as that might be for us to accept when we or our loved ones are suffering. What the devil means for evil, God turns into good.

I believe the devil saw the potential God had placed in the life of Hector. He sickened a woman's mind and led her to murder, in part, to snuff out Hector's life at an early age. But the devil lost again!

The devil may make us sick and make us suffer. But God is still greater – and he's still working out his plan.

CHAPTER 9

The Intimidation Factor

The devil's scare tactics

In my ministry, the enemy is constantly working to thwart our efforts. Everyone involved in our outreach to the inner city is quickly introduced to frontline spiritual warfare, even if they've never experienced it before. And often in ways they never imagined were possible. When you assault Satan on his own turf, you can always expect a struggle.

But a different dynamic occurs whenever I'm called to write about the enemy's tactics. His attacks suddenly become far more brutal and private. I'm not sure why. I can only guess that this somehow feels more personal to him, more insulting and permanent. Perhaps more damaging to his ego. After all, it was pride that brought him down in the first place.

Whatever the reason, the effects are very real. And everyone involved begins to experience it.

This truth became evident to me years ago, while I was writing *Satan on the Loose*, my first book on spiritual warfare. The attacks I suffered during that period were some of the most frightening of my life. Many of them still haunt my memory.

It's true that the devil's attempts to scare me don't have anything like the effect they had before I knew Christ. Now I know more about the devil, and now I have the power of the Holy Spirit inside me, I am equipped to respond to my enemy with the weapons God gives. But his attempts at harassment are troubling just the same. He loves to frighten. He is the ultimate terrorist.

Stories of the Past

The attacks began at the earliest stages of writing *Satan on the Loose*. I had decided to make a trip to Puerto Rico to interview my mother about her experiences with witchcraft. As I described in an earlier chapter, Mama had become involved in witchcraft, sorcery and other practices after marrying my father. But since giving her life to Jesus several years earlier, she'd had nothing more to do with witchcraft. She didn't even like talking about it, but I knew she'd be willing to do so if it would help me with my book. She'd do anything to keep just one soul from being ensnared by evil.

The publishing company brought several people out to meet me in Puerto Rico, including an editor from *Christian Life* magazine. They wanted to sit in on our interview so they could meet my mother and take notes.

It was a clear, bright day in Puerto Rico as we pulled up the driveway to our small home in Las Piedras. All of the editors were with me, and the five of us stood on the porch as I knocked on the door. I had expected Mama to answer, but instead my sister, Carmen, opened the door to let us in. I made all the introductions and then Carmen said, 'Mama is very sick. She was feeling fine a few days ago, but she's been in bed sick the past two days. We have no idea what's wrong.' Knowing what I now know about the devil's ability to afflict people with illness, it's not hard to imagine that he sent this illness to discourage my mother from participating in the interview. (She later recovered fully.)

My mother knew that I was coming and had been looking forward to our visit. I stood in the living room praying silently, wondering what we were going to do, when suddenly Mama appeared in the doorway. She looked pale and weak, but she came out to greet us anyway. I told her we could reschedule the meeting, but she insisted that we sit down with her on the porch and visit. Mama was a strong woman.

We spent hours laughing and visiting with Mama on the small porch outside our home. The editors would ask Mama a question, and I would translate as she answered in Spanish. A tape recorder sat on the middle of the table and one of the editors kept a close eye on it, reversing and changing the tape as needed.

With a beautiful disposition, Mama told story after story of the many strange and frightening things that had happened in our home through the years because of her and Papa's involvement with witchcraft and sorcery. It was interesting to hear her perspective on so many of the strange and unexplainable events that occurred in my childhood – things I remembered well yet never fully understood. Many of them I had tried to forget.

As I sat and listened to Mama's stories, I couldn't believe that this was the same woman I had grown up with – the mother I had grown up fearing. I couldn't believe that this was the same person who had treated me with such anger and hostility, who had once called me a 'child of the devil', who had brought so much harm and turmoil into our home through her evil spiritual practices. This woman before me was nothing like that. This woman was loving and joyful and beautiful. Mama had been completely transformed by the blood of Jesus and the power of the Holy Spirit.

Useless Tapes

Before we knew it, the sun was starting to set. None of us wanted to tear ourselves away from Mama's infectious smile and captivating laughter, but I could tell she was getting tired. So I ended the meeting and helped Mama back to her bedroom. 'Thank you for your help,' I told her as I tucked her under the covers. 'A lot of people will be helped by your insights.'

As I was in my room later that evening, I got a call from one of the editors. He had been testing the tapes and noticed that there was a problem with nearly every one of them. One tape was completely blank and another began tearing and winding its way through the recorder as he tried to play it. Several others were nearly inaudible. Most of the material we had gathered was gone forever. 'I can't understand what happened,' he told me. 'This has never happened to me before.'

I was so discouraged and frustrated by this news that I didn't even eat dinner that evening. I just wanted to slip into bed and try to get to sleep. I was wondering how I'd ever remember some of the stories Mama had told in such detail. I couldn't believe that all our work had been lost.

As I lay there, though, a boldness came over me and I began to address the enemy. 'Enough is enough! You are not going to stop me from writing this book. You are not going to discourage me from moving forward! I don't care what you do, I'm going to hurt and expose you for the coward you are, not just in this book, but in everything I do! I've dedicated my life to exposing your lies, and nothing you do can stop me!'

Even in the midst of my holy anger, I knew that his subversive attacks had only begun. Indeed, the deeper we dived into the manuscript, the more blatant the enemy's assaults became. Let me tell you of just one more incident.

Spontaneous Ignition

Towards the end of the project, I was working late one night in my rented office in Raleigh, North Carolina, going over some final revisions to the manuscript. From my office window I could see the lights of the city twinkling in the distance as far as the eye could see.

At about 11 that evening, I completed my revisions and dropped the manuscript into my briefcase. I gathered my things and walked outside to the parking lot, pulling the car keys from my pocket. I couldn't wait to see Gloria and tell her I had finally finished work on the book.

But as I approached the car I noticed a strange noise. It was coming from underneath the hood. And the closer I came, the louder it seemed. Suddenly I realised what it was: the engine was running.

I glanced down at the keys in my hand, then back at the car. No one was inside. The doors were still locked tightly, yet the car was running! *How could this be? How could it start by itself?* (Keep in mind that, back when this happened, there was no such thing as keyless entry or remote start!)

For several seconds I just stood, stunned and staring at the car. Wondering what could have caused this strange occurrence. Wondering what I should do. Instinctively I realised that it was another of the enemy's attacks, another supernatural event meant to frighten me.

I began to pray, at first in silence and then aloud. 'Jesus, help me know what to do. Give me the strength to over-come this attack!'

Then I started yelling at the devil. 'You can't frighten me! I'm not going to be intimidated by you or any of your demons or any of your tactics!' Finally I called on Jesus himself to handle this attack.

I unlocked the door, then climbed into the driver's seat and slipped the key into the ignition. But before I could turn it, the key fell to the floor! The car had rejected it. I reached down and picked it up, then slipped it back into the ignition. Again it was rejected! Five more times I did this, and each time the key was pushed out of the ignition from the inside, as if some force within the steering wheel were pushing it away.

I paused for a moment to gather my courage. I was not going to let this destroy me mentally or spiritually. I had always been a fighter and I would not let Satan conquer me in this moment.

At that instant I jammed the key into the ignition and turned it, before the ignition had time to push it away. The engine died. I quickly took the key back out. My hands were shaking and sweat was running down my cheeks. I'd been claiming that I wasn't frightened, but the truth is, it was one of the most terrifying events I'd experienced in a long time – even since my childhood experiences with the supernatural.

I got out of the car and went back upstairs to my office and called Gloria. My voice was shaking as I told her what had just happened.

'Wait there,' she said. 'I'll come get you.'

I wasn't about to argue.

I went into the bathroom and splashed water on my face. My muscles were tight with tension. My hands were still trembling. I tried to tell myself that the event was over, that the enemy couldn't harm me, no matter how hard he tried. But somehow the fact that he had been able to take control of my car was more than I was prepared for. *What if he was able to take control while I was driving?* I thought. *What if he could do the same with Gloria? If he can take over my car, what else can he do?*

Soon Gloria arrived to take me home. She laid one hand on my shoulder and prayed for me as we drove, pleading the blood of Jesus over me, claiming protection from the evil one. Together we were strengthened.

The Devil's Leash

In spite of Gloria's prayers, I hardly slept that night. I lay awake for hours pleading with God to give me a sense of peace and comfort – to assure me that my family would be safe from the assaults of evil. I needed to know that the enemy would not be allowed to hurt us. That he was not as fierce or frightening or powerful as he felt to me that evening, as I had sat helplessly in my car, trying to take control back from the evil spirit that taunted me that night.

I knew the day of my conversion that I was no longer a bastard; I had a heavenly Father who would take care of me. And I needed my Father in this moment.

As I prayed, a strange sense of calm began to fill my mind and spirit. In my heart, I sensed God saying, *Nicky, you know you have nothing to worry about. You know I won't let any harm come to you or your family or anyone else working with you on this book. The adversary may feel frightening, but he is nothing. He has no authority over my children. I will never let him bring you harm.*

At that instant God brought Philippians 4:7 to my mind. 'The peace of God, which transcends all understanding, will guard your hearts and your minds in Christ Jesus.' It was a consoling thought. And it made perfect sense to me. The prince of darkness cannot enter the castle of my mind; only the Prince of Peace reigns there. After all, God 'has rescued us from the dominion of darkness and brought us into the kingdom of the Son he loves'.[1]

I pledged to never again let the enemy get an upper hand over my emotions. He had tried to deter me from God's plan for my life, to frighten me into losing sight of the goal God had in mind, but it didn't work. God's hand of comfort calmed my fear and brought clarity. Despite the damaged tapes and the self-starting car, I finished *Satan on the Loose*, and I and my family were fine.

Satan is a master at making himself look more powerful and deadly than he really is. He knows how to lie and deceive us into thinking that he is someone to be feared – that his power is great and his bite poisonous. But in reality he is like a junkyard dog, chained to a fence. He snarls and snaps and bites, intimidating through fear and threats. But he can't do any more harm than God allows. He can't reach us, because God has his leash firmly in his hand.

Don't get me wrong: if we get too close to evil and are not walking with the Spirit of Christ, the devil can certainly deceive us and lead us astray. That's why experimenting with evil is such a dangerous preoccupation, as I said in Chapter 4. It leads us deeper and deeper inside the enemy's territory, and the nearer we walk, the more vulnerable we become. He can do untold damage to those who dare to draw too near.

But for those who choose to stay away, he holds little threat. His barks are nothing to fear. He can't touch those of us who stay safely inside the protection of God's loving arms!

A Lion with False Teeth

I once got a call from John Sherrill, a good friend and writer I've known for years. At the time I was working on another one of my books, and he warned me to be prepared for spiritual opposition. 'Satan usually strikes us at our weakest points,' he said, 'and you never know what he might try.'

John told me that he had recently been working on a book about demonic oppression, when every appliance in his house went haywire – all at the same time. And many of them were new. It was far too strange to chalk up to chance.

He prayed for me over the phone, asking God's blessing on my writing, and I'll never forget the words he used. 'Lord, help us remember that although Satan goes about like a roaring lion, he has false teeth. And when we submit to God and resist Satan, he has to flee.'

What an important truth for Christians to remember! We need to constantly remind ourselves that Satan has no power over those who are covered in the blood of Jesus. He can tempt and taunt us, but ultimately he has no more bite than God allows him to have.

That doesn't keep him from working to hurt us. It doesn't keep him from attacking at every opportunity. It doesn't keep him from trying to frighten and discourage us. But we just mustn't give in to fear. This is what I've tried to live by and what I teach others.

Years ago, my daughter Nicole, now a doctor of psychology, was researching our family history for her thesis. When she learned more about my parents' involvement in spiritism and some of the wicked things I had participated in as a young man, she became very concerned. She asked me if she and my other children and grandchildren were going to suffer for 'the sins of the fathers', as the Bible puts it.[2] Was she going to be a victim of a generational curse? She was really quite frightened at this prospect.

I told her and all my other daughters, 'No! The curse was broken on the day of my salvation. There is no curse on my children and grandchildren.'

When the enemy tries to plant a seed of fear using voices or shadows or whatever, we can't let it grow by letting our minds dwell on it. We cannot allow fear to overcome us. We are the property of Jesus Christ! Let us dwell on him, and the fear inside will shrivel and die.

CHAPTER 10

Unwelcome Guests

Demon possession and oppression

I've already told you how evil spirits would possess my mother in the Spirit House behind our home in Puerto Rico. And I've told you how demons would nearly press the breath out of me when I was lying in bed as a boy in Puerto Rico and again as a young man in Pennsylvania. Now I'm wondering about your reaction to all of this. Our rationalist world tells us that so-called demon possession is a fraud or hysteria or misdiagnosed mental illness. Do you believe that? Or do you believe demon possession is real?

Of course there *can* be false identifications of demon possession. And sadly, I've seen instances where Christians have imagined they've seen demonic activity in all sorts of places where it didn't exist. We can easily go overboard if we're not careful. If you take this book as incitement to go on a demon hunt, you've really misunderstood me!

Nevertheless, I assure you that demons are real. Just as there is a God, so there is a devil. Just as there is heaven, so there is hell. Just as there are angels, so there are demons. The Bible is full of cases of demonic influence, possession and exorcism.[1] And on a personal level, I can tell you that I've seen more examples of possession in my life than I could possibly tell you about. Many more.

For example, my sister, Carmen, was possessed once when she was a child. I watched as an evil spirit changed her behaviour and even her appearance from the inside. I saw her eyes glow orange. Her face became unbelievably distorted.

It hurt my father to see his only daughter in that condition. He tried every ritual he could think of to remove the demon from his child but he was unable to do so. He didn't have access to the power of Christ then; he only had his sorcery to rely on, and that wasn't enough. Finally the demon left Carmen by its own volition, after a three-week possession.

More recently I was preaching to an audience in a hall that was full to overflowing at the University of Lyons, France. I'd been speaking about the dangers of witchcraft and the crowd of thousands had been hanging on my words. After issuing an altar call, I was expecting many to come to Christ. But just then, from about five rows back, a well-dressed man in his forties suddenly stood up and started barking loudly like a dog!

I immediately sensed the tension in the crowd. I knew this was a demonic manifestation. And I knew that, if I didn't do something quickly, this man was going to destroy the chance that so many had to enter into eternal life.

Using the authority given by Christ, I pointed my finger straight at the man and shouted, 'Shut up and fall!' I bet you can guess what happened. That's right – he emitted one last little howl and fell to the floor. As much as he tried to get up, he couldn't move.

Everyone was shocked at what had happened, but many came forward with tears in their eyes. The demonstration of Christ's power over demons had cemented their resolve to know him. I'm told that, even after the rest of the crowd left the hall, the barking man still couldn't get up off the floor!

Demon possession may be happening much more often than we believe. What about the serial killer David Berkowitz – the 'Son of Sam'? He has said that he belonged to a satanic cult and that he was instructed to kill by a demon that inhabited his neighbour's dog. Or what about Andrea Yates, the Houston mom who drowned her five children in a bathtub? She testified that she heard voices and saw visions, that Satan commanded her to kill her children.

Demon possession, in fact, can crop up almost anywhere, even in unexpected places. Jesus encountered a demon in a synagogue. I encountered one in a church.

The Devil's Altar Call

One day, in the late 1980s, I was scheduled to speak at a church in California. I expected it to be an ordinary speaking event for me. It proved to be anything but.

I had met the pastor before (I'll call him Arnold), but when I got to the church, I noticed that something was different about him. Arnold seemed arrogant, disconnected. He had a hard time looking me in the eyes. Had I just caught him on an off day? I didn't think so. I sensed that there was something wrong on the spiritual plane, perhaps something seriously wrong.

That evening I began preaching. It's hard for me to describe what happened to me then, but it felt like the words I was preaching kept bouncing back at me. I was preaching the same kind of message I normally did, but it was going nowhere. I kept thinking, *What is going on?* I began to realise that a spiritual problem in the room was affecting me in the pulpit.

And I was not the only one who sensed the spiritual conflict. Jeff Fenholt – a Christian performer best known for playing the lead in *Jesus Christ Superstar* on Broadway – was there helping me with the event. He told me later that he also felt something was spiritually wrong from the start.

Somehow I managed to get through the sermon. Then came the altar call. It was the hardest one I have ever given in my life. There's nothing I love better than inviting people to come and experience the love of Jesus, but this time I had trouble getting the words out. And the people resisted – no one came forward to the front of the sanctuary. The men and women remained in their pews, looking uncomfortable. Again I thought, *What is going on?*

That's when events took the strangest turn of all. Finally someone did come forward, a man from the congregation. But he did not want to receive Christ – far from it. His eyes were glowing orange, just like my sister's eyes when she was possessed as a child. His face was distorted and filled with hate. He didn't even look human.

There was no doubt now: the spiritual battle I'd been sensing was one with demons. And a demon was now openly manifesting itself in this man.

I was shocked, but there was no way I was going to let the demon have its way! I went up to the man and started praying for God to send the demon away. The pastor did nothing to help me, choosing to hang back. But Jeff Fenholt joined me and started praying. (You can imagine what the people in the congregation were thinking by this time!)

For some reason the man fixated on Jeff. Activated by the demon inside him, he hissed, 'He's mine. I'm taking him to hell with me.' Then suddenly the man spat at Jeff, following up by saying, 'I've given you AIDS.'

Jeff was understandably concerned, but I told him not to accept what the demon had said. We prayed for Jeff's protection, and I told him to go and wash off the spittle.

The battle went on as others came up to help me. It took ten men to hold the demon-possessed man down and then carry him to another room, where we prayed for his release. In the meantime, we asked the congregation to keep up a flow of praise and worship in the sanctuary – after all, evil spirits hate the worship of God! After an hour and a half, the demon finally left the man.

We found out later that Pastor Arnold had become deeply involved in adultery and other forms of sin. That accounted for the odd behaviour I had noticed. I firmly believe that the sin situation in the pastor's life had enabled demons not only to influence him but also to infiltrate his church.

After his sin came to light, Pastor Arnold was counselled and offered restoration. But I'm sorry to say that he eventually gave in to his flesh, losing his wife and kids in the process.

Possession vs Oppression

I'm often asked if Christians can be possessed by demons. The answer is no. As believers, we are indwelt by the Holy Spirit and he will not share space with unholy spirits. Only people who have never yet trusted in Christ, or who have renounced him and walked away from him, are susceptible to being possessed. Christians can, however, be *oppressed* by demons. Rather than being inhabited on the inside by demons, we are attacked by them from the outside.

I believe that what I witnessed in that California church illustrates both kinds of influence by demons. The pastor was a believer, but he had let himself wander far from Christ and had opened himself up to the effects of demons. And through this opening, demons had gone into a man in the congregation.

So, what does it all add up to? On the one hand, we don't need to fear demon possession for ourselves. If we are walking with the Lord, no demon has access to take over our lives. But on the other hand, we need to know that we are not immune to outward influence by demons. They can oppress us, and it's not an easy thing to go through.

There are many forms that oppression can take. If we are being oppressed by demons, we may witness disturbing phenomena. We may live in bondage to fear, confusion or uncontrollable emotions. We may struggle again and again with unholy fantasies. Evil spirits are not inside us, using us for their own purposes, but they may be close to us, trying to get us to think or feel or do what our Lord would never approve.

We should do our best to identify demonic oppression carefully. For example, just as oppression is not the same as possession, so oppression is not the same as depression. Oppression might feel like depression, but depression has different causes and different cures. Medication can help depression and should be used. But a spiritual solution is called for when the cause of what we feel is a spiritual attack.

And while I'm at it, let me make one other distinction. The suffering that is caused by oppression is generally not on a par with the torment that the demon-possessed undergo. The Lord protects us from that. One demon-possessed man in Jesus' day was so miserable that he lived in a cemetery, crying out and cutting himself with stones (not unlike the self-injury of 'cutters' in our day). He was hopeless and wretched until Jesus showed up to rescue him.[2] The suffering of the oppressed is not that bad. But it is bad enough.

We can fend off attacks by being strong in the Lord and, with God's help, not giving the devil any opening.

Laying Out the Bait

One of the devil's chief activities is to tempt us. It's been that way ever since Eve and the forbidden fruit.[3] The devil can't force us to sin. But he can present us with the opportunities to sin and then add his thoughts to our own to make the sin look attractive to us. He works with the world (the sinful systems all around us) and the flesh (our sinful nature) to get us to take the bait.

Now, it's important to keep in mind that being tempted is not a sin in itself. If it were, the sinless Son of God would never have been tempted – yet he was.[4] Rather, we sin when we give in to temptation. It's up to us: will we be like Eve, who went along with the serpent, or will we be like Jesus, who rejected every offer Satan made? Our joy and effectiveness for the Lord hang in the balance. This is why we must pray, 'Lead us not into temptation, but deliver us from the evil one.'[5]

Sin is wrong in itself. It is also dangerous in that it makes us more susceptible to demonic influence. As we've already seen, dabbling with danger through participating in such things as the occult can open a way for the demonic to enter our lives. And the same is true of sin in general: it makes us vulnerable to oppression by the dark dominion.

Of course, demonic oppression is not always a sign that a Christian is involved in sin. For example, when I was attacked by a demon on the day after my baptism, that wasn't my fault. It wasn't due to some recent sin in my life. As I said in Chapter 6, I believe that the devil was making a final great attempt to pull me back to his side.

But, often, demonic oppression *is* due to sin. That's what happened in the life of that California pastor. It's what's happened in many another Christian's life. I've known Christians, for example, who thought it was no big deal to go to parties where drugs were being used or wife swapping was taking place. But such environments are favourable to evil spirits. Indulging in sin like this opens us up to their activity in our lives. We have to say no to temptation.

The apostle Paul put all this in spiritual warfare terms, urging us to put on the armour of light:

> The hour has come for you to wake up from your slumber, because our salvation is nearer now than when we first believed. The night is nearly over; the day is almost here. So let us put aside the deeds of darkness and put on the armour of light. Let us behave decently, as in the daytime, not in orgies and drunkenness, not in sexual immorality and debauchery, not in dissension and jealousy. Rather, clothe yourselves with the Lord Jesus Christ, and do not think about how to gratify the desires of the sinful nature.[6]

Let us be serious about holiness. Leaving behind sin means distancing ourselves from the devil and making ourselves less vulnerable to demonic oppression.

Still, protecting ourselves from oppression is only half the story. What are we to do when we meet *others* who are either possessed or oppressed by demons?

Exorcism 101

Let's say we meet someone who just seems evil. Maybe we can't quite put our finger on it, but we sense a spiritual presence within them that is not godly. Or maybe this spiritual presence gives the game away, openly manifesting supernatural behaviour or blaspheming God through the human's voice.

Or let's say we've met a fellow Christian who doesn't seem right to us. They betray anxiety, perhaps strong fear. If we bring up spiritual matters, this person changes the subject. They justify their sin. They seem immune to the Holy Spirit.

In the first case, we might be faced with a demon-possessed person. In the second, it might be a demon-oppressed person. But either way the question is, what will we do about it?

Run away – right? Well, we might want to. But let me speak frankly with you. Imagine me looking you straight in the eyes as I say this to you: *Each of us, if we are believers in Christ, is able to help in releasing the other person from demonic influence.*

Right now, maybe you're thinking, Oh no, Nicky's trying to turn me into an exorcist. Images of holding up a crucifix or flicking holy water are appearing in your mind.

Relax.

For one thing, God might never call us to intervene in such a spiritually charged situation. But then again, like Jeff Fenholt and those ten volunteers at the California church, we might need to get involved some time when we least expect it. None of us has to be a pastor or priest to help in this way.

We also don't have to have special training, follow a particular formula or use any gimmicks. Casting out demons or pushing back oppression comes through praying and fasting – activities all of us believers are familiar with. We seek God for his power and then we command the demons to leave. Anyone with faith in Jesus can do it.[7]

Most importantly, it's not us who are casting out a demon. After all, we don't have the power! It's God who's doing it, and he's involving us in the process, not because he's weak but because he has given us the authority. We can call on the name of Jesus, relying on the power of the blood of Jesus, to cast out demons. God will do the work.

Jesus specifically gave his twelve disciples the authority to drive out evil spirits.[8] And when a larger group of his followers came back from a mission outreach, they said to him with joy and wonder, 'Lord, even the demons submit to us in your name.'

He agreed with them, saying, 'I saw Satan fall like lightning from heaven. I have given you authority to trample on snakes and scorpions and to overcome all the power of the enemy; nothing will harm you. However, do not rejoice that the spirits submit to you, but rejoice that your names are written in heaven.'[9]

Because the power is God's, and our authority comes from him, there is no excuse for pride. Neither is there any excuse for shrinking back in fear. The same authority that was given to the first followers of Christ is given to you and me.

I don't want to scare you. And honestly, I'd like to spare you having to go through a spiritual power encounter, because I've been through it myself many times and have never enjoyed it. But the fact is, through Christ, any of us can release others from the hold that evil spirits have on them. Of course, this is best done, not alone, but with other believers. And as God puts that kind of situation in front of us, then bringing his power to bear for another is both the obedient and the compassionate thing to do.

Remember that if you ever see someone's eyes glowing orange.

CHAPTER 11

Fishing Two Inches from Hell

Christians in an anti-Christian culture

In 2005, police and officials in London asked my organisation, Nicky Cruz Outreach, to hold an event in the boroughs of Hackney and Waltham Forest, where knife crimes were on the rise. They were impressed by our ministry to street gangs and prisons and were eager to see us help out in these troubled boroughs. This event was to be underwritten by the London police, with the support of Scotland Yard, and by many London area churches.

We were glad to accept this invitation. And so in the summer of 2006 we spent an extended period of time in London, holding our hit-and-run street meetings (meetings set up on the street with music, break-dancing and short testimonies) and counselling individuals with the help of three hundred volunteers from among the local Christianity community.

Each time we held a street outreach, crowds would gather to hear what we had to say. There was always a palpable sense of danger. Onetime a gang member threatened my son-in-law Patrick, saying he had a gun. I was certain he would have shot Patrick had there not been a crowd standing nearby.

In spite of this kind of thing, though, people were being touched by the truth of God's Word. At each outreach event, dozens would come forward to accept Christ as their Saviour. We saw gang members and leaders, pimps, prostitutes, drug addicts and dealers surrendering themselves to God. It was an amazing thing to witness.

But it was also clear that the forces of hell were set against us.

Just a few weeks into our outreach, the press and certain factions within the community began to turn on us. And the primary reason seemed to be the issue of homosexuality.

A Brawl I Never Asked For

Gay rights was a contentious topic in London that year, and some people, hearing that we were coming, wanted to know what our position on the matter was. A member of a group that was working with us posted a document on our website explaining what God says about homosexuality in Romans 1. This only fanned the controversy, and by the time I arrived in London, I was already labelled a 'homophobe'. And from then on, as much as I would have wished otherwise, opposition from gay rights supporters became a major issue for us.

One reporter from a local paper tried to infiltrate our group in order to trap us. During a conversation with a member of our volunteer team, the reporter began asking what the Bible says about homosexuality. The young man told him exactly what the Bible teaches – that though we are expected to love homosexuals, God condemns the homosexual lifestyle. Afterwards he was called into the police station and questioned about his beliefs. They told him it was voluntary, but he felt tremendous pressure to appear.

During another instance, several Christians decided to attend a gay pride parade just to pray on the sidelines. They did nothing wrong, yet the police quickly arrested the entire group – simply for praying!

Several times during our street outreach events, gay and lesbian activists showed up in order to cause trouble. They had no interest in talking or hearing about God; they simply wanted to argue and disrupt our meetings.

Our main outreach event was scheduled to be held at the Ocean Nightclub in East London, a popular venue for concerts. But our reservation of the facility was revoked (temporarily, I'm glad to say) because of the controversy over our supposedly homophobic views.

All of this was disturbing. But after all, it was coming from unbelievers. What upset me most was the reaction I got from certain members of the clergy. High-profile church leaders wanted me to openly condone the gay life-style, since gays in London were putting so much pressure on the Christian community. Several times they came to our team and asked that we make a public statement renouncing the biblical view of homosexuality.

But I refused to compromise. I was there to preach the

Word of God, not to water it down. I will never apologise for my convictions or dilute the commandments of God.

Initially, I was discouraged by what seemed a capitulation on the part of the Christian community. Thankfully, though, many solid Christian leaders and lay-people stood by our side. It was encouraging to see our TRUCE team standing strong in their beliefs, in spite of the pressure to give in. They did a tremendous job!

Each time a story ran in the paper condemning our biblical position on homosexuality, Christians would write letters to the editor defending us. They proclaimed the gospel boldly and clearly in their letters. And they continued to encourage us in spite of the opposition.

My publishers in the UK – Hodder & Stoughton and Integrity Europe – were a huge help to us, putting together an e-mail campaign in order to raise support from churches and individuals across Europe. It grew into an international campaign, the volume of which clogged the servers of a local paper and the city council. They encouraged believers to contact media and community leaders in Hackney in support of our outreach. At times it felt like we were in the middle of a bare-knuckle brawl between those who stood for us and those who stood against us.

Satan did all he could to discourage us, but it wasn't going to work!

Spiritual Drift

Of course, the point I'm trying to make here isn't about homosexuality. That was just the particular issue that arose for me in London a few years ago. The point is that the truths and principles of God are under attack in our world. And where's the attack coming from? You're right – it's straight from hell.

In the West, the devil has inspired a steady shift away from our society's Christian foundation. It's been happening for a long time, but in recent years it has become especially noticeable. That's what was underlying the opposition I faced over the issue of homosexuality in London. It surprised me, but I guess it shouldn't have.

I love the UK and have always considered it my home away from home. Over the past forty years, I've made forty-five tours in the UK, reaching hundreds of cities, towns and villages. Tens of thousands have responded at the altars. Many have gone on to labour for Jesus Christ in pulpits all around Europe and beyond. My autobiography, *Run Baby Run*, continues to be widely read in most of the state schools in the UK. It has also appeared in the Christian Top Ten best-seller lists every year since it was released in 1969. The people here have always been gracious and loving towards me. But something in the culture is changing.

Today there is a strong movement in the UK to silence Christians. There is little tolerance for those who claim faith in Jesus. In fact, there have been several attempts by the British Parliament to pass laws that might make it a crime to read from the Bible in public. There is pressure for it to be considered a 'hate crime' when someone shares his faith with others. Recently, I read about an advertising campaign where an atheist group raised over £60,000 to put up ads on London buses that said, 'There is probably no God. Now stop worrying and enjoy your life.'

Beyond the UK, most countries on the European continent are similarly 'post-Christian'. Some countries, including France and Germany, have fewer than 2 or 3 per cent of the population who claim to be born again. There are entire communities and regions without a Bible-believing church in sight. As I am writing this, a Turkish organisation in Amsterdam has started construction of a controversial mosque without government permission. The mosque is intended to be one of the largest in Europe. The number of Muslim adherents is growing while the Church of the Lord seems to be on the ropes and dying. Recently, the Council of Europe passed a resolution entitled 'The Dangers of Creationism in Education'. Among other troubling things, the resolution describes those who believe what the Bible teaches as 'extremists'. May the Lord of the harvest raise up new labourers who will go into the mission field of Europe – in my opinion, one of the top two or three neediest and darkest areas in the world.

Now, if you're in America you could say, 'Sure, Europe's going off the deep end, spiritually. But the United States is not like that.' And you'd be partially right. The UK and Europe *are* further along the path towards secularisation than are many other places. But I can tell you from experience that my beloved home country, the United States, is not far behind.

Circle of Stones

My office has a view that looks across the rugged front range of the Colorado Rockies. And right there, occupying one of the most beautiful tracts of land, is the United States Air Force Academy. When the weather is good, I can see the aluminium peaks of the academy's iconic chapel shining in the sun. What could be a prouder symbol of the Judeo-Christian heritage at the heart of American culture?

But half hidden in the woods nearby is a very different worship centre. It's a double circle of boulders where a handful of cadets and officers carry out Wiccan and Druidic rituals on Monday nights as well as at the spring equinox and other times of the year that are significant within the occult belief system. The site was constructed in 2010, the Air Force saying that America's principle of religious liberty required it to accommodate neo-pagan personnel the same as Protestants, Catholics and Jews.

There were protests from Christians when the 'earth-centred spirituality' site was proposed. But even in the famously Christian-oriented city of Colorado Springs, located adjacent to the academy, the protests were surprisingly muted. And moreover, these protests were nothing compared to the rhetoric that cropped up when something happened shortly after the Wiccan circle was created: someone propped a cross made of railroad ties against one of the boulders.

Tech. Sgt Brandon Longcrier, a self-described pagan who sponsors the group that worships there, said the incident was similar to someone leaving a pentagram at the academy's chapel altar. He claimed that he and others were victims of a hate crime.

And it seems the Air Force officials agreed. The academy's superintendent, Lt. Gen. Mike Gould, said in a prepared statement, 'We are taking this incident very seriously and conducting an inquiry. We absolutely do not stand for any type of destructive behaviour or disrespect for human dignity.'

Hate crime? Destructive behaviour? That's what we now call erecting a cross? What a new world we have entered!

It is not my intention to argue the case of whether the Air Force should have permitted the neo-pagan site to be constructed. I'm merely pointing out the deep inroads that other belief systems have made into American society. All across what used to be known as Christendom, in fact, culture is shifting away from Christ and towards Satan.

The Prince of This World

I've said that *The Devil Has No Mother* is so badly needed today because Christians are becoming more and more ignorant about – and apathetic towards – the threat posed by the devil. But if we look at it from a broader perspective, we can see that the Church is really just drifting with the tide of our culture on this matter. In the West, belief in God, familiarity with the Bible and acceptance of Judeo-Christian morality are becoming more and more rare. This causes us to lose sight of the devil – even though he is the engineer behind it all!

It's true that, in some sense, Satan has always been the ruler of this fallen world.[1] But his rule is becoming more clear-cut in the Western world now. That means we're living in a dangerous place, or in 'evil times', as I put it in an earlier chapter.

The father of lies wants to separate us from the truth whenever possible. We need to wake up to what is happening and not just accept the assumptions of our society. We'll be challenged to give up on our biblical principles. If we hold to the truths of the Word, we can expect more opposition than ever.

Will we take the route of accommodation? I know it would be easier. It would have been easier for me to water down my teaching when London's gay rights proponents got me in their sights. But I refused to compromise, and I pray that the rest of the Church will do the same.

I often describe how David Wilkerson, pregnant with a burden from heaven, came into the war zone that was my New York neighbourhood so many years ago. It was as if he had decided to park himself two inches from hell and then started fishing. He had no idea what he would catch; he simply kept coming back persistently with the message that Jesus loved us.

Nowadays we don't have to go onto gang turf to feel like we are aliens in a dangerous place. Our whole society is becoming more and more like enemy territory. As we hold out God's message of acceptance to the lost, we are all fishing two inches from hell.

But God's Word gives us encouragement to stand for godly truth against an increasingly devilish culture. The Lord's faithful followers have had to do something of the same throughout history, and God has supernaturally shown up to overpower the evil one.

Standing on the Truth

The Bible is filled with stories of men and women who suffered tremendous opposition for their faith.

One day, Peter and other apostles were imprisoned for preaching the truth of Jesus. And when they miraculously escaped, the soldiers once again brought them before the Sanhedrin, Israel's supreme court. The Sanhedrin threatened them with death if they didn't stop preaching about Jesus. Yet they refused to compromise. 'We must obey God rather than men!' they cried out.[2]

Paul was continually persecuted for preaching the truth of Christ. He was repeatedly beaten and scorned and threatened by those who were offended by the message of the gospel.[3] Yet he never compromised. He told Timothy, 'Everyone who wants to live a godly life in Christ Jesus will be persecuted.'[4]

And in one of my favourite stories in the Bible, Shadrach, Meshach and Abednego came up against untold pressure from King Nebuchadnezzar, the ruler of Babylon, to compromise on their convictions. Nebuchadnezzar commanded them to bow down before his golden idol or be thrown into a blazing furnace of fire. All around them God's people were bending to the pressure in order to save their own lives, yet these three men of God refused to give in.

'O Nebuchadnezzar,' they said, 'we do not need to defend ourselves before you in this matter. If we are thrown into the blazing furnace, the God we serve is able to save us from it, and he will rescue us from your hand, O king. But even if he does not, we want you to know, O king, that we will not serve your gods or worship the image of gold you have set up.'[5]

They chose to face death rather than yield to the pressures of the world. They trusted that God would save them from the fire, but they also knew that God might have allowed them to be martyred for their convictions. They hoped that God would intervene, but stood willing to follow him even to their death.

How easy it would have been for them to fold beneath the pressure. I'm sure their friends were saying to them, 'Just bow before the statue. You don't have to mean it. That way, you can live another day to worship the one true God.' All around them people were bending their principles in order to stay alive. Yet Shadrach, Meshach and Abednego refused to give in. They refused to compromise. They refused to water down the truth of God's Word.

Isn't that how God wants you and me to live in an ungodly society? Isn't that the kind of followers of Jesus we ought to be?

Jesus loves us so much that, if it were required, he would go to hell to rescue even one of us. His total commitment to his mission inspires our total commitment to standing with him.

As the 'prince of this world' seems to take more control everywhere in society, we must remember that God remains the true sovereign. He is King! The devil's domain is soon to shrink down to the size of a lake of fire.

CHAPTER 12

Relentless

The never-ending battle of evil vs good

I have to admit, I'm not a young man anymore. My days as a gang member were over more than half a century ago. I've been working in the Lord's service for a long time now, travelling all around the world. And you might think that, after all these years, I would be done with spiritual warfare. The devil should leave me alone and move on to trouble somebody else.

Is that going to happen? Hardly!

The truth is, the devil never stops attacking. He's always roaming around, looking for weak spots, trying out different strategies. As long as we're alive in this world, we're vulnerable to the vicious efforts of the devil. It just keeps coming.

I've already told you about some of the more dramatic attacks I've suffered at the hands of the devil. Now I want to begin this chapter by telling you about one of the more seemingly ordinary attacks I suffered. I want to do this because we mistake a lot of the devil's antics for 'bad luck' or 'poor timing' or simply the coincidences of life. And clearly, not all difficulties can be attributed to a satanic attack. But when you've battled the enemy as long as I have, and in the ways that I've battled him, you begin to see patterns of assaults that are impossible to explain away as mere happenstance.

An Attempt to Divert

Recently, Gloria and I were in Puerto Rico, London and Scotland doing a series of crusades. Many people came to Christ during that time. We could feel the Spirit of God moving among us at every venue. But just a few days before we were scheduled to return, I heard some disappointing news over the phone from our daughter Laura.

Laura and her family had stopped at our home in Colorado on their way from California to Virginia. They arrived late one night and the next morning noticed water damage on a wall. Upon further inspection, they found a big leak behind the TV in the family room. Laura's husband, Brian, quickly turned off the water to the house, but the damage had been done. The carpet was ruined, as were much of the plasterboard and the floorboards throughout that entire level. The water had even trickled down to the basement.

They called a plumber, who eventually determined the cause. During a remodel several years earlier, a carpenter had put a nail through the plasterboard and it had punctured a water pipe. The nail had held the water back for years but eventually rusted through. The pipe 'just happened' to burst while we were away from home on one of our longer trips overseas, thus doing far more damage than it normally would have done. The estimate for repair ran into the thousands.

We returned home and began the process of getting the damage fixed. Much of the plasterboard and many floorboards had to be replaced and repainted, and some of the wood floors had to be replaced. All that was left to do was replace the carpet in several rooms. But we had to put the remaining work on hold while we made a week-long trip to Guatemala for another crusade.

We were returning from that trip exactly thirty days from the date of the earlier damage when we got another phone call – this one from Patrick, our son-in-law. 'You won't believe this, Nicky,' he told me. 'Your house is flooded again.'

My heart sank as I heard the news. We arrived home to find the entire basement under several inches of water. This time the damage was blamed on a pipe that froze and burst during the night. All the repair work we had just done was in vain. Worse, the destruction this time was greater than the first time. This time they said that the water had damaged the slab of the house. It took months before the repairs and problems with the insurance company were resolved.

Two water problems during two ministry trips. Coincidence? Bad luck? I don't think so. It had every appearance to me of an attempt by the enemy to distract us from the fruitful work going on in our crusades. In fact, I'm sure of it.

Thankfully, this attack was relatively minor, since no one was hurt. It's when I hear of the devil's more brutal assaults on people, especially the young and innocent, that my spirit seethes with anger. One such story came my way during our outreach crusade in Scotland.

'Devil Child'

I was praying for people at the front of the Magnum Theatre in Irvine, Scotland, when I noticed a young boy. He looked to be about eleven years old. He was crying, standing at the foot of the stage where I was standing. He said his name was Nathan, and he had come forward for altar ministry.

I asked one of the new converts to lift him up onto the stage, where I pulled him close in order to pray for him. His little arms wrapped around my waist and held on tight. I prayed a wall of fire around him, and I whispered into his ear how I wished that someone had prayed for me when I was his age.

Little did I know at the time the depth of pain that he'd already experienced in his young life. It wasn't until his mother e-mailed us to say thanks that I found out what God had actually done that night for Nathan.

Nathan had been through more trauma and terror in his eleven short years than I have time to describe. His father had grown up in St Lucia, in the Caribbean, and had been heavily influenced by voodoo and sorcery. The dad's childhood had been marked by beatings, torture, abandonment and demonic visions, and now he tormented Nathan and Nathan's mother with cruel abuse that never let up.

In the midst of all this, Nathan's mother, Catherine, cried out to God for help. She writes, 'I wasn't a Christian at this point but had a Bible and used to pray that God would help me. God was my only friend in all of this.'

It always moves me to hear about people calling on God for help, even before they are saved, because he always hears and always responds. He cares! Jeremiah 29:13 says, 'You will seek me and find me when you search for me with all your heart.' He also promises to be close to the broken-hearted and those who are crushed in spirit.[1] And he was listening to Catherine, although things didn't immediately improve.

Let me share the rest of her e-mail with you:

We moved to South London when Nathan was almost three. I hoped that a new place would be better for us, but it just got worse. There were periods of time when I would get a little break from the beatings, and I learned to say all the right things. I tried to keep Nathan quiet and occupied so he wouldn't be a target for violence. I remember one day Nathan took a big slap from his father round his little face. The imprint was red and speckled with blood under the surface. Unfortunately, there was more to come.

His father was obsessed with the devil and the wrongs that had been done to him throughout life. He used to speak of a group of witches who attacked the house where he lived with his grandmother. There were lots of stories of demon manifestations and of terror, murder and ill treatment. During this time he got hold of some magic books. A door had been opened, and it was at this time that he started seeing the dead walking.

Nathan was growing up into a happy little boy with a soft heart. His father hated this and said he was a devil child because he made too much noise and was stupid. He seemed to rain down pain and coldness on any good feeling or expression of love. Nathan's father didn't know how to love, for he had not received any himself.

All these long years I felt that God had not answered my prayers, but he was working in our lives all that time. I didn't give up, and the breakthrough came when I asked for deliverance and made plans to go to a women's shelter, where we were finally free.

Thankfully, this story has a happy ending. When I met Martin, my husband, Nathan took to him right away and enjoyed playing and the positive attention. His [emotional state] has gotten a lot better, although I have been told that the devil had such a strong hold on the father that he will try and come for Nathan as well. God is good and he will protect us, I have no doubt. So it was no coincidence that we should be at Nicky's outreach on Sunday. Nathan had a lot buried in him and it was time to let go, praise God. This is enormously significant as Nathan's future will be changed from this – the power of forgiveness is truly amazing. Now that he has God's covering, there can be nothing greater than that, and he has come a long way through prayer and an outpouring of the Holy Spirit on our family. Sunday with Nicky was so incredibly significant.

When I read these words, I am hit with a flood of emotions. I remember the terror and abuse that I endured as a boy and the rejection I felt. I wince as I read those terrible words: *devil child*. I can imagine Catherine's feelings of frustration and hopelessness, because that was my experience as well, although in a different situation. I can feel the joy and healing and release all over again as the reality of the healing power of Christ washed over my life, changing it forever. What Satan meant for evil in my life, the Lord turned into good. He will do the same for Nathan.

I praise God for this brave young man, whose spirit so obviously has been touched by the hand of God and who knows, even at eleven years old, the amazing power and freedom in forgiving an abuser. I knew that night that what God was doing in Nathan's life was going to redefine his future. God has only begun to do great things with him.

Nathan, may you be mighty in his kingdom!

Relentless in Battling Evil

The attacks from the dark side may be severe or may be more minor. They may come one right after another or take a temporary break. But they never really stop. They are a part of our story throughout life, and they continue from one generation to the next.

I understand that this might seem discouraging. But I am determined to tell the truth about the devil in this book, and his relentlessness in pursuing our destruction is a part of the truth.

God never discharges us from his army. We've got to be

prepared to fight our enemy, not just for a while, but for a lifetime. We've got to be determined. Persistent. Ever vigilant. We have to be as relentless as Satan is.

And there is reason for hope. More than hope – steely confidence! After all, God has promised that he will never leave us or forsake us. And as we will soon see in many ways, the one who is in us is so much greater than he who is in the world.[2]

So take heart! As a man who has walked with Jesus for more than half a century, I can tell you that God renews the strength of those who turn to him. He will uphold you as you fight for his kingdom.

A Grim Summary

Now, before we move on, let's take a moment to review what we've learned about the devil.

Chapter 3:
Even though many of us have all but forgotten about the devil, he is alive and active today. We're bound to come up against examples of his activity from time to time. The truth is, we live in evil times – and it seems like they may just be getting more evil than ever.

Chapter 4:
The devil provides gateways to draw us deeper into his clutches. Dabbling with the occult and other ungodly things is very dangerous, yet many people – both believers and unbelievers – are doing just that.

Chapter 5:
The devil wants us to think we are trapped. He tries to deceive us into believing there is no way out of loneliness, addiction or whatever trouble we're facing. And if we believe his lies, we really do stay trapped.

Chapter 6:
The subject of the devil is no abstract topic. Demons sometimes personally attack individuals. And let's face it: their power is strong – much stronger than our own strength.

Chapter 7:
The devil tries to masquerade as being better than he is. He looks like light, but he is darkness. If we saw Satan for who he is, we wouldn't want to have anything to do with him.

Chapter 8:
The devil hates us. And within limits set by God, he afflicts people both mentally and physically. To the extent that we give place to the devil, he takes advantage of it.

Chapter 9:
The devil loves fear, and so he tries to scare us. Particularly when we are attacking him directly or doing something that interferes with his wicked schemes, Satan causes manifestations designed to frighten us.

Chapter 10:
The devil or his spirit followers, the demons, sometimes possess unbelievers. They cannot possess believers, but

they can – and do – oppress us, especially if we have gotten tangled up in sin.

Chapter 11:
Our whole society is shifting from God's side to the devil's. The ground under us is changing, so that we are standing on alien turf. Just as he is being taken less seriously, the devil is more and more asserting his rulership over this world.

Finally, as we have seen in this chapter, the devil just keeps on attacking us in small and large ways. We're never discharged from the Lord's army. If we're alive, we still have a commission to fight.

My friend, this is what you get when you face the devil. *'Ese hombre no tiene madre.'* This is why we have to wake up and see that we have a real enemy who is powerful and horrible. We can't underestimate what he's capable of.

But I hope you remember the other side of the story . . .

Foretastes of the Final Victory

We've learned some other things so far, some much more hopeful things:

- Yes, Satan is alive and active in these evil times.
  BUT – God is still in control and working out his great plan.
- Dabbling in the occult and ungodly forms of entertainment exposes us to spiritual danger.

BUT – as we abandon those foolish activities, we close the doors on the gateways to the demonic.
- The devil has brilliant powers of deception to make us feel trapped.
  BUT – Jesus is still in the business of setting people free.
- The devil and his demons attack us individually.
  BUT – the blood of Jesus protects us.
- Satan masquerades as an angel of light.
  BUT – God's Word shows us that the devil's realm is a dominion of darkness.
- The devil afflicts us with mental and spiritual harm.
  BUT – God redeems what the devil tries to destroy.
- The devil finds creepy ways to scare us.
  BUT – he is like a junkyard dog: he's kept on a leash by God.
- The devil possesses and oppresses people.
  BUT – as we stay close to God and reject temptations to sin, we can successfully resist demonic influence.
- The devil is tilting our whole culture his way.
  BUT – God enables us to stand up against evil in our society, and he remains in ultimate control.
- The devil just keeps attacking.
  BUT – God will help us to hold firm for as long as we need to.

This is a much more positive picture, isn't it? As I've been saying since the beginning of the book, there isn't even a contest when it comes to the devil's power versus God's. Our Lord's greatness is always more than enough, and he gives us confidence of victory.

For the rest of the book, we will be looking at ways that God gives victory. And ways that we can participate in his defeat of the devil in our day.

This is where it gets fun.

PART 3

God

The one who is in you is greater than the one who is in the world.

(I John 4:4)

CHAPTER 13

Setting Captives Free

God's grace available to all

When Nicky Cruz Outreach held a crusade in El Salvador a few years ago, a man known as El Viejo Lin – 'The Old Man' – heard we were coming. An inmate of a prison in El Salvador, he held the position of president of the Eighteenth Street gang in that country. He was called 'The Old Man', not because he was actually old (he was only about thirty), but because of his position of leadership within his gang organisation. He was certainly not a Christian. Far from it. But he had heard about me and evidently respected my life story. He ordered his entire gang to attend my crusade. Ten thousand members of Eighteenth Street tried to get into my speaking sessions, though the police allowed only three thousand of them in the doors. Many of these gang members received Christ, including El Viejo Lin's fiancée, Graciela.

I thought that might be the last I would hear of El Viejo Lin. But not so. He called our host ministry in El Salvador and asked if I would come to speak in his prison. This prison had just been through a brutal riot, and several of the prisoners had been killed. Hoping that I would bring some peace to the prison, he wondered if I'd be willing to come and speak to the inmates.

Of course I said I would. As soon as I could get some time available, I was headed back to El Salvador.

To the Inner Court of Hell

When my companions and I arrived by helicopter, we found that the prison was located deep in the mountainous countryside of El Salvador. It had a foreboding appearance, with brick walls surrounded by steel gates and barbed-wire fences. It was a maximum-security prison, one of the most heavily guarded in all of Central America. This is where they put some of the most dangerous men in the region.

Inside, the supervisor in charge ushered us through many parts of the prison. But most of what we were seeing seemed to be office areas and lunch rooms and guard stations. We saw hardly any prisoners, though we could hear them in the distance. I turned to the supervisor and asked, 'Where do you keep the inmates?'

'They're kept in the centre of the compound,' she told me. 'But you don't want to go there. It's not safe. We'll bring some of the prisoners to visit with you in the outer-court area.'

'Take me there,' I told her. 'I want to go where the prisoners hang out.'

She told me again that it wasn't safe in the centre of the compound. I could tell she was nervous – and I knew she was feeling that way for a good reason. I had learned that, just three weeks earlier, a Catholic priest had been held hostage by the prisoners for four days. This was clearly not a safe place to be. 'Even the guards don't go there,' the supervisor said. But I insisted, so she eventually agreed.

As we moved towards the inner-court area, the shouts and laughs of the inmates grew louder. The iron bars clanged shut behind us at every station, each one guarded by several armed officers, huge men with bulging muscles and stern eyes. It was obvious they took their jobs seriously. Where we were going was a frightening place – that was becoming more evident by the minute. But in my heart I had no fear. I knew that God would never allow me to be harmed. He never has.

We turned a final corner, passed by several more heavily armed guards, walked through one last set of thick steel doors, and suddenly found ourselves standing in the middle of the inner-court compound. Hundreds of prisoners stood staring at us. Men were pacing back and forth in the courtyard, whispering among themselves as we ventured into their territory. Several of them bunched together to one side, fixing their gaze firmly upon us, as if we had crossed some sort of sacred line.

Every one of them seemed to be covered with tattoos – on their necks, arms, shoulders, hands, even the sides of their heads. Several had shaved heads and full beards. I recognised many of the tattoos as gang symbols, most from the Eighteenth Street gang, one of the largest and most notorious gangs in the world. It began in Los Angeles and soon spread into other countries, including Central America. Today the Eighteenth Street gang, along with their allies, the MS-13 gang (*Mara Salvatrucha*) have a combined membership of approximately eight hundred thousand in the United States and seventy thousand in Central America. They are some of the most vicious criminals on the planet, ruling the streets with an iron fist. Even inside prisons they dominate through fear and intimidation, and their presence here was clear the moment I walked in.

The area grew deathly quiet. The roar of noise we heard from the hallway was now nothing but a gentle murmur. You could tell they weren't used to having visitors, at least not in this part of the prison. Not in the inner compound, the belly of the beast.

Even Dracula and Frankenstein would fear to enter this inner court!

The Spirit Comes to the Prison

I stepped forward and stood in the middle of the yard, with inmates on every side. For some reason, I was alone with the prisoners – no guards, no warden. Even before I said a word, I could sense that the men were ready to listen. They had already heard that I would be visiting the prison that day, though I doubt they expected to see me in the centre of the compound.

'I'm not here to preach to you out of the Bible,' I told them. 'You've probably heard that all your life. And I'm not here to tell you that you're sinners, because you already know that. I'm just here to tell you my story. I want to tell you what Jesus has done in my life, and you decide what to do with it.'

Then I told them my testimony – a story I've shared thousands of times in my life yet never tire of telling. That's because it's the most powerful tool God has given me. It's the one thing that can't be debated or ignored. You can argue with someone's opinion, but you can't argue with their story. What God has done in my life is a miracle too great and powerful to deny.

The longer I shared, the more I felt God's power. I could feel the presence of evil subside as the inmates received my testimony. The feeling of darkness and oppression was slowly being replaced by a sense of calmness and peace. God's Spirit was moving among us, softening hearts, bringing souls to conviction. Several of the inmates bowed their heads in reflection; others fought back tears. It was an awesome thing to witness.

As I prayed for the prisoners, I sensed a strong chorus of repentance coming from many hearts. Even some of the hardest criminals, the ones who had remained along the edges of the inner compound throughout my visit, standing with their arms folded and hearts guarded, even they grew quiet and reflective. God was working in their hearts, pleading with them to give in to his mercy, beckoning them to accept his free offer of salvation.

Only God knows how many souls were saved that morning. And how many more were simply brought one step closer to embracing the love and mercy he offers. It was clear that he was doing a mighty work within this hardened prison compound.

Never Shake Hands with the Devil

When I finished praying, several of the inmates came forward to meet me. One was the man who had called me during my crusade, El Viejo Lin. As president of the Eighteenth Street gang, he was treated with special favour and privilege by both the inmates and the guards. He had two cells to himself, a colour television and regular protection from the other inmates wherever he went.

As I was speaking with him, another man stepped forward from the centre of the courtyard. I'd been watching him from the moment we walked in. He was surrounded by about fifty inmates during my entire visit, and it was clear that he was their leader. He moved in my direction, extending his hand towards me. 'My name is El Diablo,' he said.

Diablo is the Spanish word for 'devil', so I knew that wasn't his given name. I left my hand by my side and looked him in the eye. 'No,' I said. 'I don't shake hands with the devil.'

My comment surprised him. He lowered his hand and stared hard into my eyes. A hush fell on the room. His smile faded and I could see his mind racing with confusion. The tension in the room was palpable. Everyone waited to see what would happen next.

'I have nothing to do with the devil,' I continued. 'If you want to shake hands with me, then give me your real name – the one your mother gave you.'

He glanced at the ground for a second, then gazed over his shoulder at the men watching from a short distance. After several seconds, he looked back at me and said, 'My name is Edgar.'

I took a step forward and smiled, extending my hand towards his. 'Now I'll shake hands with you,' I said, grasping his right hand firmly. I placed my left hand across his shoulder and pulled him towards me, then turned to the other men in the room. I said in a loud voice, 'From now on, I don't want any one of you to call this man El Diablo. He is not the devil. I know the devil, and this is not him. The devil hasn't got an ounce of good in him. He's more hateful and evil than any man could ever be. Even on your worst days none of you could come close. I didn't come here today to shake hands with the devil; I came here to hurt him. This man is not evil. He has a good heart – I can tell. And he should never be called the devil. I don't want any of you to ever call him that again!'

The man's eyes rose to meet mine as I turned to address him directly. 'Don't ever let anyone call you El Diablo again,' I said. 'Your name is Edgar. That's what I'm going to call you, and that's what you need to call yourself.'

He glanced down at the ground, then again brought his eyes up to meet mine. 'Yes sir, Mr Cruz. My name is Edgar.' (After that day, Edgar called our office several times, and he assured us that he continued to go by his given name.)

We talked for a while longer, then several of the other men in the room came forward to meet me. I can't remember most of the names, but I'll never forget the faces. Faces of shame, loneliness and regret, yet somehow hopeful as

143

well. These were good and decent men in many ways – men who wanted to live right, who longed to turn their lives around if they only had the chance.

I spent hours talking and praying and crying with the prisoners. Each one came to me with a different story, a different prayer need, a different reason to talk. My heart went out to them. My soul burned with compassion. I wished I could help them somehow undo their past, help them make right the things they had done to land them in prison. But I couldn't. All I could do was pray for them and tell them of God's love and mercy. It was the thing they most needed to hear.

Bittersweet News

A lot has transpired since my time at the prison in El Salvador. A few things bring mixed reaction to my spirit – encouragement and sadness at the same time.

El Viejo Lin, the 'old man' who first contacted me to speak at the prison, is still incarcerated. He and his fiancée, Graciela, had been waiting for him to be released so the two of them could marry. After she had received the Lord, she had begun attending a local church and became faithful to the Lord. But sadly she was killed in an act of gang violence and now is with Jesus. El Viejo Lin, while mourning her, remains solid in his new-found faith.

Meanwhile, Edgar, the man once known as El Diablo, was paroled soon after my visit. With the help of his wife and his church, he began ministering to gangs and speaking to groups about the dangers of the gang lifestyle. He was filled with potential and I had great hope for him.

I really thought he might be the next Nicky Cruz, a gang-leader-turned-worldwide-evangelist. But it didn't turn out that way.

I knew Edgar was at risk. Any ex-gang leader who turns to the Lord and leaves his life of crime is a target. And just as David Wilkerson protected me after my conversion by sending me to Bible college on the other side of the country, so I was working with a ministry to get Edgar and his wife out of El Salvador so they could be safe and the Lord could continue to use them. Unfortunately others did not recognise the risk.

One day Edgar was asked to speak at a school in an area where he was well known as a gang leader. It was a risky thing to do, and I would have advised him not to go, but he did. He and a missionary spoke at the school assembly, but then a group of gang members followed the two men and later that day shot them both several times, leaving them in the street to die. Edgar died instantly, and the missionary died in the hospital a few days later.

I can't tell you how much it hurt me to hear this news. If only I could have helped Edgar before he agreed to speak in such a dangerous area! But I'm comforted to know that he is now safe in the arms of Jesus.

El Viejo Lin and Edgar both discovered something very important. As much wickedness as they had been responsible for, and as strong as was the devil's hold on their lives, God's power was still more than strong enough to free them from sin and hell. This is because the greatest Warrior of them all has already sunk his sword into the devil, and the evil one is dying before our eyes.

The Deathblow

As I said at the beginning of this book, the devil has no mother. He's a hopeless case. He hates you and has an awful plan for what he wants to do in your life. He's a monster who spends every moment of his existence contemplating ways to kill, steal and destroy everything that God loves – beginning with you and me, God's precious children. He works tirelessly to tear us down and break our spirits.

But that's really only half of what this book is trying to say . . . and not even the more important half. The more important message is that God is great and powerful and active on our behalf. In his love, he is doing mighty miracles that turn back the works of the devil.

When Jesus came to earth, he came to destroy Satan's work.[1] As we have seen, he cast out demons whenever he encountered them. But those were mere skirmishes. His goal was to inflict a final defeat upon the devil. As he looked ahead toward his death, Jesus said things like 'Now is the time for judgment on this world; now the prince of this world will be driven out' and 'the prince of this world now stands condemned'.[2] And that's just what happened. The devil must have thought he'd achieved a great victory when the Son of God died upon the cross, but the victory quickly turned to defeat when three days later Jesus rose to life eternal.

Jesus strode deep into the devil's territory, just as I went into the depths of that El Salvador prison, and there he conquered the devil. This changed everything for those who believe in Jesus. No longer must the devil have free rein to drag us down into hell with himself. Now we need not fear, for we share eternal life with our Lord. This was God's intent for Jesus from the beginning:

> Since the children have flesh and blood, he too shared in their humanity so that by his death he might destroy him who holds the power of death – that is, the devil – and free those who all their lives were held in slavery by their fear of death.[3]

This is why the Easter mood should always be dominant in our lives. This is why, although we should respect the devil's power, we need not live in fear of him. The devil, despite everything in his bag of tricks, is still a defeated foe. Let me say it again: *he's already defeated!* Jesus did this. Jesus bound the 'strong man' – Satan – and is in the process of robbing him of all the precious people he has taken captive.[4]

My friend, we must believe this, take it deep into our hearts. We must learn to expect great and mighty works from God in our lives.

CHAPTER 14

Walking through the Pages of the Book of Acts

Salvation, signs, wonders and miracles shall follow

The message of *The Devil Has No Mother* is badly needed today because so many Christians have lost sight of the harm their spiritual enemy, Satan, can do. The devil is just as active today as ever, carrying out his schemes in the supernatural realm. But we don't see it. 'Devil – what devil?'

The flip side of this problem is that Christians are not seeing God at work either. This is an even more serious form of spiritual blindness. We read in the Bible about the great and mighty works he performed in ages long past, and we believe those reports, but we don't expect him to work miraculously in our day, in our lives.

Yet it's happening, if we'll only open our eyes. It's happening all around the world. And God's mighty works are the surest sign that he is in the process of defeating the devil. God's power is greater than the devil's, and when the lost are saved, the sick are healed or other miracles take place, that's God's power at work taking back ground from the enemy.

An Unwanted Invitation

Recently, Gloria and I were in California on vacation, when one evening an old friend of mine – Norman Roman – called out of the blue. He had heard that Gloria and I were in California, and he was wondering if we'd be willing to come and visit his family. At the time, Norman's family were having their annual reunion at a campground some distance away from where Gloria and I were staying. He said there were about eighty-five of them at the camp. 'They would be thrilled to see you,' he told me.

I wasn't so thrilled at the idea going to the camp. For one thing, I was exhausted from a gruelling schedule of travelling and speaking. For another, I'm a city boy at heart and really don't like hanging out in the woods. I was looking forward to resting at our hotel and had no desire to spend an hour and a half driving just to get to the campground. So I told Norman I'd have to do it another time.

After I hung up, however, Gloria went to work on me. She argued that it would be fun and encouraged me to make the trip. I grumbled and complained, but in the end I called Norman back and agreed to come for a couple of days. He thanked me for changing my mind and said he'd make the arrangements. I still didn't really want to go. But as it turns out, God had something special he wanted me there for.

Meeting Matthew

The minute Gloria and I walked into the camp, we started bonding with Norman's family. We had dinner together, then sat around a bonfire in the campground, visiting late into the evening. It had grown dark, yet none of the kids left. We were all talking and laughing, enjoying one another's company.

Then I noticed a young man standing nearby. He was tall and good-looking. There was one thing odd about him, though. He was completely bald.

Maybe I'm not always as sensitive as I should be. I just came out and said to him, 'You look like a football player. Why don't you have hair?' I assumed he had shaved his head simply because that was his chosen style. But he surprised me.

With sadness coming over his face and his voice cracking with emotion, he replied, 'Because I'm dying.'

I talked to Norman about this young man later and got the details. 'His name is Matthew,' my friend said, 'and his body is eaten up with cancer. He's only nineteen years old, but he's been through dozens of operations. They don't expect him to live long. He's been suffering with cancer since he was a child, and now there's nothing more the doctors can do.'

As Norman and I talked further, I learned that this boy was the grandson of a woman I'd known for years, Rachel Sanchez. I'd known Rachel since my days in Bible college, but I had no idea she had a grandson dying of cancer. I also learned that Rachel was attending the reunion. At that instant I felt a strong voice from God speaking into my spirit. It wasn't a soft, quiet nudging from the Holy Spirit. It was more like a firm command. A directive. God was saying to me, 'Pray for him, Nicky. I'm going to heal this boy today.'

A Prayer of Faith

It's not often I hear God speak with such clarity, but when I do, I know a miracle is about to take place. So I stood up and said to the young man very firmly, 'You are not going to die. I'm going to pray for you tonight and God is going to heal you. But first I want your grandmother to be present. Who's willing to go and get her?'

Several of the kids agreed to go after her, so we waited for them to return. The young man didn't know what to think. He sat quietly, without saying a word. I'm sure he had been prayed for many times in the past, yet God had never chosen to heal him. I didn't blame him for being sceptical.

Rachel was sombre and serious when she arrived, no doubt wondering why I had sent the kids after her. We hugged, and I briefly explained to her that we were going to pray for her grandson, and I wanted to make sure she was there with him. I could tell she was moved, yet still somewhat reserved – maybe even doubtful.

I asked everyone to gather around the campfire. Several of the kids huddled together beside the young man, laying hands on him as I started to pray.

'Dear Jesus,' I began, 'thank you for what you're going to do here tonight. Thank you for your glory and power and mercy. You are a miraculous God, and we need a miracle. I know you're going to provide one for us. Right now we call on you to come down from heaven and heal this young man. Take his cancer and burn it from his body. Satan is not going to destroy this man – he's going to live! I pray for him to be healthy in the name of Jesus Christ! I command his cancer to leave! Take his sickness and give it to the devil! Let him die with it! Send him to hell with this boy's cancer seething inside his body, because this boy is going to live!'

The crowd grew silent as I called on the blood of Jesus to bring healing to the young man and comfort to his family. I took authority over his cancer and commanded it to leave in the name of Jesus. When I finished praying, it was obvious that those around were shocked by my boldness, but I knew in my heart that God had brought me to this place for a reason. He was ready to display his power, and I was simply the vessel he chose to work through.

Rachel was in tears as she lifted her head. I wondered how many times she had bowed her head to pray for her sick grandson, yet had never seen healing. I wondered what she was thinking and feeling at this moment.

The kids surrounded the young man and hugged him, each one patting him on the back and giving him words of encouragement. We all sensed that something miraculous had happened. God's Spirit was moving among us; we could feel it, sense it within our hearts and souls. I had no doubt that God had made his body whole.

I didn't hear anything from Norman for several weeks after that, but in my heart I knew that God was going to show his power. I'm not always this certain, but something within me just knew that God had orchestrated my visit to the camp for this very reason.

Then one day our office got a call from Norman. He told me that Matthew had just been to the hospital for more tests and the doctors could find no more signs of the bone cancer. They had been treating him regularly for bone cancer, as well as a tumour, and both were completely healed. The doctors were baffled and had spent the entire day running test after test in an effort to explain what might have happened to the boy's cancer, but no explanation could be found. He was completely healed. The cancer that had been ravaging his body was entirely gone!

Signs and Wonders

No matter how often God works, I'm always amazed by his power and goodness. I don't always understand why he chooses to answer some prayers yet remains silent regarding others. I know it has nothing to do with me. I'm an evangelist, and my calling is to bring people to Jesus Christ. Healing is not my calling, but I have no control over what the Holy Spirit decides to do. He sometimes works through me, but he can also work through any believer. I have no power to bring miracles to the world; only God can do that. I just move where he leads me and pray when he leads me to pray. Yet he has given me so many glimpses into his supernatural power through the years. And for that I am humbled beyond words.

What's missing in the lives of many believers today is the belief that it can happen. And that it can happen through *us*, in *us* and around *us* by God's power.

Think about the book of Acts. Think about Peter healing the crippled beggar at the temple. Think about Peter, and later Paul and Silas, being miraculously released from prison. Think about people being healed merely by touching Paul's handkerchiefs!

Were Peter, Paul and the other early Christians who saw miracles in the time of Acts fundamentally any different from us? Like us, they were flawed human beings. Like us, they were operating in the time between Jesus' ascent to heaven and his return. Like us, they had the Holy Spirit indwelling them.

The only difference between them and those of us who are hindering God's miracles is faith. They believed that God would perform miracles, and so he did it. Somehow, along with losing a proper understanding of the devil, we've lost a belief in God's miraculous power.

But the facts are the facts: God is still a God of salvation and healing. We must believe that we can walk through the book of Acts and that we will receive the glory of the Lord like never before. All of us. With signs and wonders.

We serve a God of miracles and healing. And when he decides to act, it's our job to simply listen for his mandate and then be ready to move with him. We need to believe God for a miracle and then pray boldly for him to show his power. God desires for us to take authority over evil and shove our doubts aside, believing that he can and will work.

After all, as we've seen, he said that he gives us authority over evil spirits. He said that what we bind on earth will be bound in heaven and what we loose on earth will be loosed in heaven. We need to take him at his word. I loosed Matthew from his cancer, not through any power of my own, but through the power of Christ that commanded me with his strong voice to pray for healing. Any of us can do the same as God enables us and directs us. We must be obedient to his voice. When the Lord calls, he equips!

Now, we know that the devil loves it when people are hurting and suffering. No doubt he approved of every growth of deadly cells inside young Matthew's body – and was dismayed when God took the cancer away. The devil is always on the side of sin, sickness, injury, emotional instability, limitation and need of every kind. But the devil is up against a power greater than his own. God always takes the other side.

We defeat the devil, then, not just by playing defence through resisting his attacks, but also by going on the offensive by establishing God's kingdom through his miracle power. By not just talking about our authority or studying it or wondering about it but *using* it.

Jesus used his authority when he walked the earth, performing miracles that stunned the onlookers and horrified the devil. And he said, 'I tell you the truth, anyone who has faith in me will do what I have been doing. He will do even greater things than these, because I am going to the Father.'[1] We can do even greater things than Jesus did, because we have the power of God in us through the Holy Spirit!

Miracles weren't just for Jesus. They weren't just for the apostles. They're not just for pastors and evangelists. They are for all of us – all Christians. Believe it.

Believing is Seeing

One day Jesus sent his disciples across the lake by boat while he went to a mountainside to pray alone. Soon the winds kicked up and started tossing the boat to and fro, so Jesus decided to walk out on the water to help them. Here's how Matthew recorded what happened next:

> During the fourth watch of the night Jesus went out to them, walking on the lake. When the disciples saw him walking on the lake, they were terrified. 'It's a ghost,' they said, and cried out in fear. But Jesus immediately said to them: 'Take courage! It is I. Don't be afraid.'
>
> 'Lord, if it's you,' Peter replied, 'tell me to come to you on the water.'
>
> 'Come,' he said.[2]

Notice how the disciples responded when they saw Jesus walking towards the boat. They became terrified and cried out in fear, 'It's a ghost.'

How could they not have recognised him? How could they have been surprised that Jesus would be able to walk on water? Shouldn't they have expected him to do something this miraculous? They were in trouble, and you'd think they would have been watching for Jesus to come to their aid. Yet when they saw him, their doubts rose to the surface. 'It's a ghost,' they said. They never imagined it would be Jesus.

But Peter's reaction was different. 'Lord, if it's you,' Peter replied, 'tell me to come to you on the water.'

Peter believed in God's power. He was able to put his doubts and fears aside and say, 'This isn't a ghost; it's Jesus!' Peter saw the miracle for what it was. And because of it, he was able to walk on water along with Jesus. He didn't just see the miracle; he experienced it. He lived it. He made it a reality in his own life, not just something he witnessed in the life of someone else. Peter believed that God could help him walk on the surface of the water and because of his faith, God answered his request!

Far too often you and I are like the disciples. We want to believe, but our humanity causes us to doubt. We see God working among us in powerful ways, doing things that only God can do, yet we turn away in fear and say, 'It's just a ghost. It's not real. These things don't really happen today.'

It's not surprising that we have trouble believing such things, because Satan is a master at casting doubt. It's what he does best. 'God doesn't really do miracles today,' he whispers into our ear. 'That's just an illusion. That's not Jesus walking on the water; it's just a ghost.'

And that's all it takes to keep us in the dark.

Satan has blinded the minds of unbelievers in this world, but don't be like them. Don't let him blind your heart to the truth. God is constantly at work in the world today, and all you have to do is open your eyes to see it. His supernatural power is being displayed in the natural world on a daily basis. And he is working just as powerfully and miraculously as he did among those in the early church.

'Be strong in the Lord and in his mighty power,' said Paul.[3] God's power has not diminished. His desire to bless and provide for us is as real as it has ever been. His ability to heal the blind, to make the lame walk, to bring hearing to the deaf, to cure cancer, to do away with any and all earthly afflictions, even to raise the dead, has not gone away. He is not a ghost. God is not dead; he is alive! He is real. He is loving. He is powerful. And he hears your prayers!

Don't ever let Satan convince you otherwise. Don't ever allow the deceiver to deceive you. Don't ever doubt the power and authority of the living God.

Believe what you see, and see what you believe. It is not a ghost. It is Jesus!

CHAPTER 15

A Surprise from God

He wants to do miracles for every one of us

I said in the previous chapter that God wants to do miracles *through* you. But he also wants to do miracles *for* you.

As I say that, a desired miracle probably springs immediately to your mind. At any given time, most people need a miracle. Or if they don't, they soon will. God wants to perform such miracles for us: both ones we desire with all our hearts and ones we have never even thought about.

Receiving a miracle is one way of growing in faith and service to Christ. When we see God's power displayed in our own life, we are more ready to see his power displayed everywhere. We want to see the devil's dominion in this world pushed back so that the kingdom of God may be established, and that can only happen through God's almighty power as we join forces in prayer.

Let me tell you some stories about people who received a miracle.

Touching the Presence of God

I witnessed God's miraculous activity happening again not long ago, during a speaking engagement in Puerto Rico, my birthplace.

Before the event, I called my nephew Tato and asked him to pick me up and take me to the church building. 'And bring your beautiful wife, Arelis, along with you,' I told him. Tato is an amazing young man, but I had been worried about his spiritual life. I wasn't sure where he stood in his relationship with Christ, so I wanted him with me at the event. Something in my spirit told me he needed to be there, so I didn't give him a chance to make any excuses. If a friend had asked him, he might have declined, but with me he had no choice. I'm his uncle, so he had to say yes!

The place was completely filled when we arrived, and there was a sense of anticipation in the air. I could feel it, taste it. God's Spirit was already moving among us, even before the event began. We all sensed that something special was going to happen this evening, though we had no idea what it would be.

My sermon that evening was on the forgiveness that Christ offers. 'You never know when your life could end,' I said. 'So you need to be ready. You need to be prepared to meet Jesus face to face!'

I was completely unprepared for the response we got from the altar call. The minute I extended the offer for prayers, people started flowing towards the front of the sanctuary, weeping and calling on the name of Jesus. Soon the entire front of the church was filled with souls in need of prayer, many falling on their knees before God in repentance.

As I was praying for a young man, I looked to one side and noticed my nephew Tato. He and his wife had both come forward, and they were holding each other, weeping uncontrollably. God's Spirit had reached in and touched both of their hearts. I immediately understood why God had put it on my heart to get them here.

Then I noticed another familiar face in the crowd. It belonged to Ismael Miranda, a famous salsa singer from Puerto Rico. He had come with his wife, Janis, that evening and both of them were in tears. His wife fell gracefully on her face, weeping and praying for God's renewal. For the longest time she lay flat on the ground, as if she were unconscious. God was doing a miraculous work in her heart. Both of them were humbly open to whatever the Lord wanted for them and were completely overcome by the power of God's presence.

The pastor of the church, Alex DeCastro, said to me, 'We can almost touch God right now,' and I knew exactly what he meant. God's Spirit was as strong and commanding as I had ever experienced. He engulfed the room with his love. At one point I stood at the front of the altar and silently closed my eyes, drinking in the full breadth and depth of his presence. I could literally feel his embrace around my spirit.

I opened my eyes to complete quiet and stillness in the room. No one was moving. People stood like statues, each mesmerised by God's presence. Some stood weeping, while others simply closed their eyes and let God minister to their spirits. Many were praying. It was a sight to behold – hundreds of tender souls, standing naked and unashamed before God, each caught up in the overwhelming love of his embrace.

I want to confess, it was one of the most glorious moments I have ever experienced. My dear nephew and his wife were saved that night. There is no way I can express what a miracle that was for me and my family. It was tremendous. The whole situation was. The Spirit of God was so powerful in that place that *I* wanted to get saved that night! The salvation of the human soul is the greatest miracle we can ever witness.

A Second Wave of the Miraculous

And the miracles weren't done yet. While people remained at the front, God spoke to my spirit in an undeniable way, confirming something he had told me earlier. I made my way to the microphone.

'God wants to do something here tonight that none of us expected,' I said. 'God is going to give us a surprise tonight. He instructed me to tell you that there will be tremendous healing in this place. God wants to heal, so we're going to obey. And this isn't the kind of healing you might think. If you have a headache, I have aspirin in the car for you. What God wants to do is take broken and diseased bodies and make them well. I'm not going to lay hands on anyone, because this will be God. Some of you came here tonight with terminal illnesses, convinced that you're going to die. But God has other plans for you. God wants to make you whole again. If you have faith and believe that God can heal you, come forward right now. God is going to do a miraculous work in this place tonight, and we need to believe that he can do it! If you need prayer, come forward and let God heal you!'

Immediately I noticed a young boy of about ten making his way to the front. He was pale and white, with no hair on his head. His eyes were dark and hollow. Listless eyes. He barely had the energy to make the short walk to the altar. His mother was by his side, a young woman with desperation in her eyes. Sadness and fear weighed heavily on her face.

'My son is dying,' she said to me. 'He has a tumour in his brain and it's cancerous. The doctors say that he'll be gone in two months.' This was like Matthew Sanchez all over again. Here was another young boy, with so much life that should be ahead of him.

Tears poured from the mother's eyes as she told me of her son's sickness. But through the tears I could see the faith and hope in her spirit. She truly believed that God could heal her son. And she wanted desperately to believe that he would.

'They say I'll never see my boy again – ' she began to say.

In the middle of her sentence I interrupted her. 'No!' I said. 'No, no, no! Don't believe that! Your son will live. His time is not yet finished!' God had spoken that to my heart right then.

Then I said, 'This is God's moment! You and I have no control over what happens right now, and this sickness has no power in the presence of God!' Then I began to pray.

163

I prayed that God would reach in and take away the tumour. That he would take away the pain and sickness that had plagued this child of God. That he would remove the tumour and give this young man a strong body and strong bones and a long and fruitful life. I prayed for God to reveal the full extent of his love for them through a miraculous healing. It was a prayer as bold and confident as I had ever prayed. I knew in my spirit that God had orchestrated this moment and that he was going to reveal his power to this young man and his weary mother. Her faith was great, and he was going to reward that faith with a miracle.

That night I went to bed knowing that God had done a miraculous work in the lives of those who had come. I prayed silently for the ones who had come for healing, especially the young man and his mother. In the depth of my spirit I knew that God had heard and answered their prayers.

Doctors Confounded

It was several weeks before I arrived back in my office in Colorado Springs. The first day I got back, I received a call from my nephew Tato – the one who had come to Jesus that night in Puerto Rico. He could hardly articulate his words through his excitement. 'Tio,' he said, calling me 'Uncle' in Spanish, 'we're still talking about what happened at the service. People are calling me every day, still connected with Jesus in a way they never felt before. And you'll never believe what happened! Remember the boy you prayed for?'

'Yes, I do,' I told him. 'He's the one I remember the most.'

'Well, he's healed! He's been to the doctor four times and they can't find anything wrong with him. The first time he went, the doctors didn't believe it, so they told him to come back again. The next time, they searched every inch of his body and couldn't find a hint of cancer! It's completely gone from his brain. The doctor asked his mother, "What happened? What medicine did you give him?" She told them it was the power of prayer – that God had healed him!'

Even as he spoke, I found myself thanking God for his goodness and mercy. I was so excited to hear the good news of what God had done. I wished I could have been there when the doctor told the mother that her son was whole again. I wished I could have seen her face as she realised for the first time that her prayers of faith had been answered. She will never again doubt God's power. And this brave young man will go on to be a living testament to God's unwavering love and his complete dominion over the natural world.

Hope for the Hopeless

As I spend my days travelling and ministering around the globe, I run across people every day who are anxiously waiting on some kind of help from God. Some are simply longing for a word from God, just to know that he's there. They need to know that he hasn't forgotten them. Others are in desperate need of a medical miracle. Their bodies are weak and ravaged with sickness, and they cry out to

God for healing. Still others have come to the end of their rope and simply need God to rescue them. They're often on the brink of bankruptcy or divorce or even suicide, and they come to God as their last and only hope. Through a series of poor life choices they've found themselves living in hell on earth, longing for just a glimpse of heaven.

These are the kinds of traps and afflictions I have said the devil places on us. They move us towards destruction and death, when God would move us towards wholeness and life. And while we're dealing with these issues, the suffering can be intense.

So people come to me and ask me to go before God on their behalf, somehow believing that my prayers will get God's attention, even though their own prayers seem to have fallen on deaf ears. They think that maybe if I lay my hands on them as I pray, or plead with God loudly enough, he will finally come to their rescue. Somewhere in their spirit they wonder if I don't have some kind of pipeline to heaven that isn't available to the average believer. How ridiculous!

I always direct people to stretch their faith and believe that anything can happen when the Holy Spirit works. There's nothing wrong with asking others to pray for you. But there's nothing magical about it either. Each of us can pray for ourselves.

And in that moment, God responds. The floodgates of heaven burst open and he brings the full force of his healing touch into our lives. His helping hand reaches into the natural world, bringing supernatural health and restoration to those who are lost and lonely and broken-hearted.

'Blessed are the poor in spirit, for theirs is the kingdom of heaven,' said Jesus.[1] And I've seen that promise from God played out more times than I could count. Wherever you find people who are broken and hurting and spiritually bankrupt, God is right there with them, waiting to usher them into his mighty kingdom.

I'm fully convinced that every person on this planet has a miracle in their life that God is waiting to perform. A prayer that God is longing to answer.

And all the while God is waiting to display his power in his time. Waiting to reveal his mercy. Waiting to bring comfort or revelation or healing. Waiting to reach into the natural world with supernatural peace and clarity.

God is waiting to do a miracle in *your* life. It may not be the miracle you expect, and sometimes isn't the miracle you've been praying for, but it is always the miracle you most need. Believe in this truth, believe in God's power, believe that he can and will help you in your time of need, and allow yourself to discover the unmistakable love and provision of God. Believe that your prayers can be answered.

CHAPTER 16

Miracle on the Eighth Floor

Faith as the catalyst for miracles

One time, Jesus was preaching in his hometown of Nazareth when the people started expressing their doubts about his divine nature. All over Israel, this man healed the sick, cast out demons, calmed storms, multiplied food and even raised the dead, but in Nazareth the people did not believe in him. And so 'he did not do many miracles there because of their lack of faith'.[1] The Nazarenes missed out.

On another occasion, Jesus' disciples failed to cast a demon out of a boy who was suffering greatly. They asked the Lord, 'Why couldn't we drive it out?'

Jesus replied, 'Because you have so little faith. I tell you the truth, if you have faith as small as a mustard seed, you can say to this mountain, "Move from here to there" and it will move. Nothing will be impossible for you.'[2]

Could it be that a lack of faith on our part is hindering the Lord's work to counteract the devil's plans in our day? And on the other hand, if we had more faith, might we see a massive outpouring of God's power to establish his great works?

I don't claim to have extraordinary faith. And I certainly understand that I don't possess any supernatural powers on my own. But on the other hand, I have seen God do great things so many times over the years that I have learned to believe him if he whispers in my heart that he's going to perform a miracle. That's exactly what happened one time not long ago when a man I knew named Steve Vergo was lying sick in the hospital.

Steve and Kathie

Steve was in the hospital, struggling through a series of near-fatal health problems. He'd been through an emergency abdominal surgery and, while recovering, he had suffered a massive haemorrhagic stroke, leaving the entire left side of his body paralysed. The doctors had just moved him to the rehab floor of the hospital, preparing him for the possibility of being dependent on his wife and four children for the rest of his life. He couldn't walk or dress himself or even eat without help. He was still a young man and he was struggling to accept the fact that he might be an invalid for the rest of his days.

Steve was the husband of a beautiful Christian woman who at that time worked in our office – Kathie. Her husband's decline had happened so rapidly that she didn't have time to absorb even one piece of it before the next round of bad news would come. In the beginning, before it was decided that he had suffered a stroke, he was being prepped for brain surgery to look for an abscess. Kathie was told to get Steve's living will in place and was warned that she would likely have to have their three-level home remodelled before Steve could be released by the therapist. Steve had suffered memory loss. At one point Steve's vision was a concern as well. Each time Kathie called the office, there seemed to be more bad news.

It broke my heart to see what Kathie and Steve were going through.

What Eyes of Faith Saw

One day, when Steve had been in the hospital for more than three weeks, Gloria and I were driving home from church, when the Lord spoke to my spirit. His voice was clear, whispering into the depths of my heart. He told me I should go to the hospital to see Steve.

We quickly turned the car around and headed to the hospital.

Steve was lying motionless in the hospital bed when we walked into the room. His face was thin and pale, his eyes serious. He could barely turn his head to greet us. His dear friend, Pastor Gary Lipich, was standing beside his bed. The room was deathly quiet, except for the steady buzz of the monitors.

We visited for a short while with Pastor Lipich. Then, all of a sudden, Steve began to open up to me. Although he was a believer, he was also something of a workaholic, and now that he'd had so much time alone to think and pray, the Lord had been convicting his spirit. 'I've been spending so much time at work that I've neglected my family,' he cried. 'I can see how I have put work before God and my family. I think that may be why God allowed this to happen to me. It was the only way he could get my attention.'

It was clear that his remorse was genuine and that he desperately needed to talk to someone. So I just waited and listened.

Meanwhile, as Steve was confessing to me, a voice rose up in my spirit. The Lord was speaking to my heart, saying, 'Pray for him, Nicky. I'm going to heal him today.'

Seeing Steve lying there helpless in his hospital bed, it seemed almost crazy to think that he might be healed. But that's seeing with natural eyes only. There are also the eyes of faith, and they showed me something else. I believed God really would heal this young man.

Pastor Lipich, Gloria and I gathered around Steve's bed as I laid hands on him and began to pray. 'Lord,' I said, 'you know that Steve's heart is genuine. He understands the things he's done wrong and he's pledged to do better. He understands why you allowed this sickness to come over him. He knows what he needs to do in order to change. And I know that he'll do that. But now, Lord, we're asking for healing. You said you have given us power over sickness and death, and right now we claim that power! Come into Steve's body and heal him. Strengthen his muscles and bones. Display your power here today, Lord, and make Steve whole. In the name of Jesus, I command this sickness to leave!'

By the time I finished praying, I felt so much power and emotion that I was laying my entire upper body across

Steve's chest. I could literally feel the power of God working in Steve's heart!

Steve was fighting back tears. His lip was trembling and his eyes were swollen and red.

I patted him once more on the shoulder. 'It's going to be fine, Steve,' I told him. 'God is going to heal you.'

Then Gloria and I left the room.

Steve's Second Chance

By the time Gloria and I reached our home, the phone was already ringing. Kathie was calling from the hospital and she could hardly contain herself. She told us that she had just arrived at the hospital and something miraculous was happening. Steve was beginning to move his limbs! I had to laugh at her excitement, and I asked her why she sounded so surprised. Of course Steve was moving. God was healing him!

She explained to us that right after we left his room the physiotherapist arrived to give Steve his daily treatment. Since the doctors didn't think Steve would ever walk or dress himself on his own, therapists had been spending each afternoon teaching Kathie how to bathe and care for him. This therapist was waiting for Kathie to arrive, visiting with Pastor Lipich, when suddenly Steve moved his left hand. No one could believe it. So they asked him to do it again – and he did! He told them that the feeling in his body was starting to return.

Steve described the sensation as a warm feeling over his entire body. 'It's like I felt when I was a little boy and my mother would hug me,' he said.

172

By the time Kathie arrived, the place was already buzzing with excitement. Steve was crying and praising God as she moved to his side. He pleaded with her to forgive him for being such a distant father and husband. 'Things are going to be different from now on,' he told her. 'God is giving me a second chance, and I'm not going to take it for granted.' Steve and Kathie prayed together that day for the first time in a long time.

Throughout the day, Steve's body continued to grow stronger. He said he wanted to try and stand and, though the therapist told him it wouldn't work, he insisted on trying. So they helped him to his feet and he stood by himself. By evening he was taking steps with little help.

One week later, to the surprise of everyone, Steve walked out of the hospital and headed home to be with his family. No one could deny God's intervention in his life. God had healed him! One doctor came to see Steve just before he left the hospital, saying that he wanted to see 'the miracle on the eighth floor'.

Today, Steve is back at work, growing stronger with each passing week. He is a changed man, spending more time at home, leading his family spiritually and emotionally. God not only healed his body; he also transformed his heart.

The Power of Trust

I was thrilled when God healed Steve, just as I was when he healed Matthew Sanchez, the young man with brain cancer in Puerto Rico, and many others I have known. But let me make something clear: God does not always heal when we want him to. He remains sovereign and no matter how much faith we have we can't manipulate him into doing something he does not choose to do. Even though he always hates it when the devil afflicts people with mental or physical illness, he may have his own purposes for letting those illnesses run their course.

We have to accept that God knows best when he chooses not to heal someone or perform some other miracle that we would desperately like to see. And that kind of trust can be hard. But do you know what kind of trust I think is harder for many of us? The trust that God *will* do miracles and answer our prayers!

Too many of us are ready to make excuses for seeing no signs and wonders. What if part of the problem is our own lack of faith? What if we're like the Nazarenes and the disciples who couldn't cast out a demon – our faith wouldn't move a molehill, much less a mountain?

I believe that many times God is longing to do a miracle, yet we miss it. He calls us to step out in bold faith and take authority over sickness or evil, yet we don't pay attention to his voice. So our faith wanes. Our prayers go unanswered. Not because God doesn't want to heal, but simply because our doubts are too large for us to believe that he will.

That's just the way the devil wants us. Tentative. Timid. Doubting. After all, cowardly warriors present little threat to him.

Jesus was openly annoyed with the faithless disciples who couldn't cast out a demon. He moaned, 'O unbelieving and perverse generation, how long shall I put up with you?'[3] Let us not annoy him the same way. Let us not be an unbelieving and perverse generation of Christians but instead be a generation that trusts in God and *expects* him to work in marvellous ways, because he is a miracle-working God!

I'm convinced that every believer has moments in his or her life when God asks the believer to step out in faith. He speaks to our spirit, asking us to put away our fears and uncertainties and take a huge risk in the name of Jesus. He wants us to claim the power we have at our fingertips through the name of Jesus and believe him for a miracle, no matter how strange or inconceivable it may seem.

God whispers into the depths of our spirit, beckoning us to go further out on a limb than we've ever gone, to boldly proclaim his desire to work miracles and then to pray decisively for a miracle, fully convinced that he will follow through. Yet our fears get in the way. We push the voice aside. We ignore the Spirit's nudging and pretend it never came. Because somewhere, down deep in our hearts, we don't really believe that God will answer. We don't believe a miracle will come. So we pray silently for healing, never really expecting an answer. This is not what God wants of us.

Jesus said to his disciples, 'Have faith in God. I tell you the truth, if anyone says to this mountain, "Go, throw yourself into the sea," and does not doubt in his heart but believes that what he says will happen, it will be done for him. Therefore I tell you, whatever you ask for in prayer, believe that you have received it, and it will be yours.'[4]

James agreed with Jesus about the kind of mindset a person should have when he or she prays. 'When he asks, he must believe and not doubt.' And James went on to describe the danger in the doubting mindset. 'He who doubts is like a wave of the sea, blown and tossed by the wind. That man should not think he will receive anything from the Lord; he is a double-minded man, unstable in all he does.'[5]

Faithless prayers don't get God's attention. It is prayers lifted up in bold assurance, believing that God can and will work a miracle, that move God to act. He longs to see us put aside our doubts and fears and stand before him with nothing but an open hand and an unshakeable trust.

I have changed and matured in many ways during the decades of my Christian life. But I'm glad that in one way I haven't changed. Just like when I first came to Jesus, I believe in God so much! I am a child of God, and I believe – no, I know – that my heavenly Father can do *anything*. I've seen him do it! I hope I always have an unlimited, child-like faith in God. I hope we all do.

Paul said that God is 'able to do immeasurably more than all we ask or imagine, according to his power that is at work within us'.[6] Do we believe it?

When God wants to move a mountain, he will let us know. And when his voice comes, we should be ready, pray boldly and firmly believe that he can and will bring a miracle. The rest is up to him.

CHAPTER 17

Fighting on Our Knees

Prayer that brings down the power

In Chapter 14 I mentioned my old friend Norman Roman, whose family reunion I attended in California. But the healing of his nephew Matthew was not the first great work of God I was privileged to witness in Norman's family. In fact, the first took place in Norman's own life many years earlier.

I originally met Norman while I was still a young evangelist in the 1960s. He was a single man at the time, living a wild and rebellious life. That is, until he showed up during one of my crusades at a small church in Oakland, California.

Norman wasn't like many of the young people who would come to my outreach events. He had been raised going to church and had parents with a strong faith in God. He wasn't from a broken home. But Norman had been through a lot of pain and disappointment and he struggled to believe that God was good.

The Hardening of Norman's Heart

As a young boy, Norman spent four or five evenings a week at church. His father – known as Brother Willie – was a worship leader, and a carpenter by trade, who spent much of his time volunteering for their congregation, building pulpits or doing anything else that was needed. He was a good man, faithful to his wife and family, and a godly example to his kids. And Norman's mother, Alice, was a prayer warrior, who trusted God completely with their future. She had the unwavering faith in God that we considered in the last chapter. Meanwhile, Norman was a happy kid, and it seemed like he had everything going for him.

Then, one day, Norman's world came crashing down on him. His father was working at a construction site when the floor gave way. He fell six floors before coming to rest on a pile of twisted rubble. His body was crushed and broken beyond repair. His internal organs were still alive, so the doctors did what they could to put him back together again, but it seemed in vain. They stitched up his body with pins and needles and covered him in casts from his neck to his feet. But they held out no hope for his survival. The family was told to prepare for the worst. The doctors were certain he wouldn't live through the week.

Norman was only twelve at the time and couldn't understand why God would allow such a thing to happen. He struggled with deep anger and resentment towards God. Even though his mother remained faithful, convinced that God would heal her husband, Norman grew angrier with each passing day.

No one expected his father to survive, but somehow he held on. For more than a year Brother Willie lay in the hospital bed, his mind active but his body useless. The doctors couldn't understand what kept him alive. Meanwhile, his wife continued to pray every day that God would heal him.

At the age of fourteen, Norman felt a responsibility to quit school and take a job so he could help support the family. He spent his days picking prunes and walnuts for a nearby farmer, just to help put food on the table. They became desperately poor, surviving mostly on rice and sardines. On special occasions they would have Spam, but only as a treat.

Many nights Norman would lie in bed listening to his mother cry through the evening, pleading with God to heal her husband. She never stopped believing that God would heal him, yet nothing ever changed. His body showed no signs of improvement. And the more she prayed, the more Norman's anger seethed. He began drinking and using drugs, mostly as a way to salve the pain.

Then one day, out of nowhere, Norman's mother got a call from the hospital. Several nurses had walked into his father's room to find the cast around his chest ripped open. And he was talking for the first time in six years. They pulled away the cast to find that his muscles had miraculously begun to strengthen and grow again. It defied explanation. God was healing him!

When Norman's family heard the news, they rushed to the hospital to be by his side. The doctors said they couldn't believe what was happening. They had been convinced that he would never heal, yet here he was, talking and laughing, growing stronger by the minute.

Norman's family praised God for this miraculous healing. His mother couldn't stop thanking God for bringing her husband back to them. And the entire hospital was abuzz with excitement. The doctors and nurses were astounded by his remarkable recovery, and many came to Christ because of this miraculous event.

Even the man in the bed beside him was shedding tears of joy. The man was a former minister who had lost his faith years earlier, but because of this event, he came back to God and asked for forgiveness. He and Norman's dad travelled around the Bay Area sharing this incredible testimony. People travelled from miles around to visit Norman's family and talk to the man who had been miraculously healed by God.

But Norman's anger was too great to overcome. Even though he saw his father's recovery and wanted to believe that it was God who had healed him, his resentment wouldn't subside. His heart had become too hard and cold and distant.

The problem was that Norman was placing the blame in the wrong place. He blamed God for his father's accident and for all the trouble it had brought on the family. Even when God healed his father, Norman couldn't quit blaming God. He didn't understand that God wasn't to blame for the evil that had befallen the family – he never is. It is the devil who does harm to us and inspires the sin in our lives that multiplies evil in the world.

Norman's father was still too weak to return to work, but over the coming months and years he continued to get stronger. Still, though, Norman's anger remained. Still he wandered far from God. By now he had added the sin of sleeping with his girlfriends to the sin of drug and alcohol abuse.

That's where Norman was when he showed up that night at my crusade. He had come only because his mother pleaded with him to go to hear me speak, but his heart was far away. He had gotten high before going to church and planned to leave early for a party in San Francisco. Coming back to God was the last thing on Norman's mind.

But God clearly had other plans.

Divine Detours

I got a call from Norman's mother just before the event began. She told me a little about their family history and said that Norman had agreed to attend my crusade. She had been praying that God would use this opportunity to reach in and touch his heart, and she pleaded with me to talk to him and try to help him renew his faith. I assured her I would.

Norman sat by himself in the only available seat on the back row during the service, and when the altar call started, the pastor tapped him on the shoulder and said, 'God is speaking to you.' Norman wanted to leave, but he also didn't want to disappoint his family. So he came forward. He'd been in enough church services to know all the right things to say and do, so his repentance seemed genuine. He asked for prayers, and several of the members laid hands on him and prayed that God would take away his anger and turn him from his sinful life. His cousin heard him say, 'Yes, Jesus! Yes!' And those around him were praising God, saying, 'He's saved! He's saved!'

I walked over and asked him, 'Are you saved?'

He told me he was. But something in my spirit didn't believe him. So I said to him, 'Where are you going after the service?'

'I'm going home,' he told me.

'Good, then I'm going with you,' I responded.

He seemed surprised and stood silent for several seconds. I could tell he was searching his mind for an excuse. I can't remember what he said, but it didn't matter, because I wasn't going to take no for an answer.

I grabbed my crusade director and told him to come with us, then told Norman to take us to his car. He slowly led us out to the parking lot, still looking for a way to get out of it. It was obvious that he wanted to get rid of us, but that wasn't going to happen.

He reluctantly slid into the driver's seat of his car as I planted myself in the seat beside him. And I immediately started going through the compartments. I opened the glove box and found a bag of marijuana, so I started digging deeper, finding his pills as well. I dug through the ashtray, under the seat, between the cushions, collecting all the drugs and cigarettes I could find.

'What are you doing?' Norman asked.

But I didn't answer. I just kept rummaging through the car. When I was sure I had it all, I hopped out of the car and headed to the nearest trash can to throw it all away.

'Why did you do that?' Norman asked.

'Because you don't need any of that junk anymore,' I answered. 'All you need is Jesus.'

Norman told me later that he was afraid to interfere with what I was doing. He thought, since I had been a warlord, I might kill him if he tried to stop me. I'm sure he was thinking about all the drugs I had just thrown away and the money they had cost him. He didn't speak to us during the entire drive home, just did his best to hide his anger. But I couldn't have cared less. Norman had been angry with God for too long, and I was determined to help him see how much God cared for him.

Norman was still quiet when we reached his home, and within minutes of our arrival, he excused himself and went to his room. I still believed that God was going to work a miracle in his heart, so I didn't want to leave. Instead, my crusade director and I sat with his mother in the family room and talked. Alice was glad to see me.

I didn't know it at the time, but while we were talking in the family room, Norman was wrestling with God. He lay in the dark, thinking back on all the things that had happened to their family. About the months of seeing his dad lying in a hospital bed with no hope of survival. About the many nights when his mother lay in bed praying for his healing, believing with all her heart that God would bring her husband back to her. About the day his father miraculously came home from the hospital. He thought about all the anger and doubt that had welled up in his spirit.

For the first time since he was a child, Norman cried out to God, saying, 'I'm so sorry for the way I've acted all these years! Lord, if you are real, you know I'm not good at being faithful. But I want to believe in you. If my father's healing was from you, then touch my heart and help me believe. Heal my anger the way you healed my father! Come into my heart and help me serve you!'

At that moment, Norman felt a wave of calmness engulf his spirit. He said it was as if someone sat on his bedside and literally lifted the anger out of him. All the doubt and ugliness were gone. All the rebellion was taken from his heart. No longer was he blaming God for what the evil one was responsible for. He became a new creation!

Norman jumped out of his bed and ran downstairs to the family room. He bounced into the room, smiling and laughing, saying, 'I'm saved, Momma! I'm saved, Nicky! God saved me!' We were so startled by his behaviour that we weren't sure how to respond. But we all knew something miraculous had happened. Alice jumped from her chair and embraced him, kissing him on the cheek over and over. 'I'm so sorry for the way I've acted,' he said to her, crying in her arms. 'But things are going to be different. God has saved me!'

As the two embraced and laughed together, I knew that Norman had finally come to Jesus. Silently, I thanked God for reaching in and healing his broken spirit.

Norman glanced in my direction and I said to him, 'Now I can go home.'

Behind the Scenes

You might think the story I have just told is about Norman. Or about his miraculously healed father. Or possibly about me as his evangelist. It's not. It's about his mother, Alice, the prayer warrior.

Here's what was happening behind the scenes . . .

When Norman was a child, going to church, she was praying that he would one day know Christ in a personal way for himself.

When her husband had that awful accident, she was praying that God would heal Brother Willie and bring glory to himself.

When her husband lingered in the hospital and the family's financial needs weren't being met, the mother prayed desperately for God's intervention.

When God did finally heal her husband, she praised his name over and over.

And when Norman's continuing anger led to a disobedient, unfaithful lifestyle, she prayed, prayed, prayed for him.

She reminds me of the persistent widow in Jesus' parable who wouldn't quit pestering a judge until he granted her request. The point of the parable is that we 'should always pray and not give up'.[1]

Prayer might not seem like much, but it is at the heart of spiritual warfare. And when it comes to prayer, Norman's mother was a green beret! Believe it?

When that unfinished construction gave way and Norman's father fell six floors, reminiscent of Lucifer being cast out of heaven, don't you imagine the evil one looked on with glee at the crumpled body? And when God ripped open the father's cast, like rolling away the stone from Jesus' tomb, don't you imagine the devil consoled himself with the thought, *At least I've still got a grip on Norman's heart*?

Evil was at work there, indeed. But so was God. And in the end God took back the entire family for himself. He did it in response to the mother's faithful prayers.

Ask and it Will Be Given

As I've said before, the point is not that we can somehow control God and make him do whatever we want. He always remains in control. But as we trust in him and pray according to his will, our prayers can be answered in *amazing* ways. This is why Jesus says, 'Ask and it will be given to you.' It's why he says, 'You may ask me for anything in my name, and I will do it.'[2]

Like the persistent widow, and like Alice Roman, we can pray boldly against the works of evil and see victory because we have been given authority. We don't have the power to work miracles ourselves – that belongs to God. But we have the authority to exercise God's power in accordance with his will. And that makes us participants in frustrating the devil's plans.

Whenever we exercise our God-given authority in prayer, the downtrodden are raised up and Satan falls from his lofty place all over again. And this is something every believer can do. We don't have to be evangelists or pastors to pray with authority. Any one of us can do it, if we are a truck driver or an accountant or a convenience store clerk. Or a mom, like Mrs Roman.

We are the Church of Jesus Christ. And the gates of Hades will not stand against us, because we have been given the keys of the kingdom. Through the delegated authority of Christ, what we bind on earth will be bound in heaven and what we loose on earth will be loosed in heaven.[3] Such is the power of faithful prayer.

Group prayer is especially powerful. Just after repeating his words about binding and loosing, Jesus talked about corporate prayer: 'I tell you that if two of you on earth agree about anything you ask for, it will be done for you by my Father in heaven. For where two or three come together in my name, there am I with them.'[4] Couples and families should be praying together. Friends should be praying together. Small groups should be praying together. Churches should be praying together.

With all the churches I visit and have the privilege to speak in, I have noticed that the really successful ones have one thing in common – one foundational reason for their success. What is it? You guessed: it's prayer. All of these churches have consistent, regular times of prayer, often meeting with their only purpose being to pray.

Brooklyn Tabernacle is always packed with 3,500 praying, praising people. Times Square Church, a great praying church, is also thriving. And Christ Tabernacle in New York – what a church! They are growing and seeing sinners saved all the time because they are praying. And those examples all come from just one city. The same is true all around the world.

Prayer = power.

If you were to ask me what was the secret of cracking the shell of apparent invincibility around the devil, I would answer with one word: *prayer*. Believers in Europe, the Eastern world, America and elsewhere – we all need to meet together and pray for souls. I see no other way of bringing down the strongholds the devil has built in this world.

The evil one will be defeated by an army on its knees.

CHAPTER 18

A Glimpse of Heaven

God's timing for the soldier's release

During a busy season of our ministry a few years ago, a woman came to me with an urgent message that she said God had put on her heart. She was a woman whom I respect deeply, a godly, praying woman, so I listened carefully. She told me that God wanted me to be strong and not worry, no matter what happens, because my time was not over. 'God wants you to know that he is not finished with you yet,' she told me.

This message seemed strange to me because it hadn't even occurred to me that God might be finished with me. I had no reason to worry that I knew of. I was in good health and was aware of no particular threats to my life. So I thanked my friend for her message, but I was not sure what it meant.

A few days later, another person came to me in much the same way, with the same message. 'Your time is not over, because God is not finished with you yet,' he told me. The words were almost identical to the previous message.

Over the next few weeks, it became clear that this message was from God, because the same word came from *seven different people at seven different times*! Each person came to me out of the blue and said that God had burned this message into his or her heart. I know from experience that these things don't happen by accident or coincidence. So I began to wonder and pray for clarity. I knew that trouble must be just around the corner.

A Little Concerned

It wasn't long before I began to feel poorly. Nothing serious. Just a slight burning sensation in my chest. But I asked my wife to get me in to see Dr Greenberg, my cardiologist, just in case.

The day of the appointment came and Dr Greenberg examined me thoroughly. He ran tests to check the condition of my heart and lungs, and he took my blood pressure several times. To me it seemed like an average check-up. But I could tell from his face that something wasn't right.

After I endured a long wait in the exam room, Dr Greenberg finally came in with a serious look on his face. 'Nicky, we're a little concerned about the heart tests. I want you to come back in next week for an angiogram.'

The news wasn't what I had expected. I had felt under the weather the last few weeks, but I never imagined that something serious might be wrong with my health. I've always worked hard at taking care of my body, running several times a week and watching my diet carefully. My check-ups had always gone smoothly. So my doctor's concern this time took me by surprise.

The receptionist made an appointment for me early the following week and I made the long drive back to my office, wondering all the way what I was going to say to Gloria and my staff. It was a sobering afternoon.

A Gentle Prayer

That afternoon, sitting alone in the quiet of the living room, I slid down onto my knees and started to pray. As always, I began by praying for the many godly friends that God has brought into my life. I prayed for David Wilkerson, my spiritual father, and the church that he founded – Times Square Church in New York City. I prayed for many other friends and fellow ministers, such as Sonny Arguinzoni, Jim Cymbala, Victor Torres and Michel Durso. I prayed for Karen, our personal assistant, and other members of our staff. I prayed for Gloria and my kids and grandkids, for all my wonderful sons-in-law. And I prayed for our many good friends and neighbours around the country. I have so many people in my life to be thankful for, and I tried to remember them all by name.

As I was communing with God in thankfulness and worship, I sensed the Lord whispering to my spirit, 'Nicky, why don't you pray for yourself? You need healing.' His voice was so clear and tender. So reassuring. So gentle.

I said to him, 'Lord, I don't want to do that. You've given me everything I need. I just want to praise you and thank you. Thank you for being with me all these years. Thank you for being my Saviour. Thank you for this beautiful and private love affair that we've shared since I was a young man. Thank you for Gloria and the beautiful children and grandchildren you've given us to love and care for. I love you so much, Lord. How could I possibly ask for anything more? I have no life outside of you. You are all I need.'

As I prayed, I could feel the Lord's Spirit surround me, embracing me with his love, enveloping my heart with his hands. I started to cry. The tears came and wouldn't stop. I felt so close to him. So loved by him. My heart was throbbing with pain, but it was a good pain. Like we were connected. Like we were one.

At one point I began to think back to the message that God had been bringing to me through my friends – the seven people who had all given me the same word from the Lord. 'Your time is not over, because God is not finished with you yet,' they had told me. And suddenly I understood the message. God had been preparing me for this moment, for this trial over my health. He didn't want me to worry.

I placed my hand over my heart and said, 'Lord, my heart is yours. It always has been. I enjoy my life here on earth, but I love you so much more. I long to see you face to face. I want so badly to go home to be with you. But I know you want me to stay. You've told me that my time isn't over. Part of me is sad about that, but another part is excited about staying and continuing my work for you. I'll do whatever you want, Lord. I'm completely in your hands. Take my heart. Make it stronger if you want, or leave it as it is. This heart is yours, not mine. Just stay with me. Give me the strength to carry on.'

For the longest time I sat on my knees and basked in the glow of God's goodness. His presence was so real. So strong and yet gentle. I could feel his hand touch my heart, and it felt good.

It was a moment I will remember forever.

Vision of Glory

That night I went to bed early, hoping to get a good night's sleep, but the Lord woke me up at four the next morning. Gloria was fast asleep beside me, so I lay still, not wanting to wake her. I found myself feeling strangely sad. I wasn't sure why. I knew in my heart that God was going to take care of me, that my days were not over. He had given me a clear message that he wasn't through with me yet. But something deep inside me was still sad about that. Somehow the thought of getting to go home to the Lord had seeped into my spirit, and the idea appealed to me. I haven't been afraid of death since the day I gave my heart to Jesus, but I've also never looked forward to it. Yet now I found myself longing to be in God's arms forever. The thought of heaven was so strong and real to me.

As I lay on my back, I closed my eyes, hoping I would drift off to sleep. But I remained wide awake. My mind was active and alert. And suddenly, in my mind's eye, I began to see a vision.

I saw myself lifting off the bed and into the air. I knew I wasn't dreaming, because the vision was so vivid. It was a strange and powerful sensation. Soon I was flying through the sky, going higher and higher into the clouds. I couldn't slow down. I was travelling faster than I'd ever travelled, with nothing to hold me up, yet I wasn't afraid. I flew for what seemed an eternity, the wind and clouds rushing past me at breakneck speed. It was like nothing I had ever experienced or imagined.

Farther and farther I went, faster and faster. Soon the clouds and sky that surrounded me disappeared, and the sky was nothing but pitch black. Just an infinite span of empty space. And I was still flying, still propelling forward through space.

Suddenly, far in the distance, I saw a small light. A tiny flicker in the middle of the vast emptiness. And it grew larger as I approached. The closer I came, the more glorious and bright it appeared. Soon the skies started to light up around it, around me, enveloping all of space. As I drew near, it began to take on the shape of a huge city. I knew it was heaven. It was an enormous mass of light, floating in the middle of the universe. I'd never seen anything so breathtaking! So huge! So indescribable in its beauty! And I was heading straight towards it.

God was taking me to heaven. He was taking me home. And I was so excited, so thrilled at the thought of seeing him, so eager to stand face to face with my Lord. I could feel my heart racing, beating faster and faster, harder and harder. My mind raced with anticipation.

As I reached the entrance, my eyes scanned the huge archway towering above the front doors. The doors were massive, sparkling with brilliance. I reached out to touch them. They were solid and warm.

And closed shut.

Beside the doors was a huge button. It wasn't really a button, but that's the only way I know to describe it. It was just there, a round object that I somehow knew was meant to trigger the doors to open. So I began touching it, pushing it, grabbing it, twisting it, hitting it, trying to figure out how it worked. I knew that this was the way to get in, but I couldn't make it work. Nothing I did seemed to help. No matter how hard I tried, or how long I fiddled with the button, the doors wouldn't open.

Just then a voice boomed around me, a voice so large and loud that it seemed to shake the heavens. A voice that I'll never forget. It said, 'Nicky, you can't come in. Go back! It's not your time.'

I pleaded with the voice. 'Please, just let me see inside. I want so much to see you, God! Why can't I stay?'

I continued to hit and push and twist the button, but nothing happened. I was frantic to get inside. Then the voice came again. 'Go back, Nicky. You are not yet finished.'

At that instant I opened my eyes and I was back in bed, lying beside Gloria in the darkness. My heart was still beating fast and my mind was still racing. I started to cry. I couldn't help myself. I so much wanted to go inside the doors of heaven, to be with my Father. But the vision was gone.

As I lay in bed, I tried to bring the images back, to somehow recapture the mental picture and complete my journey. But I couldn't do it. And I was so sad. So disappointed. So depressed that I wasn't able to travel farther into that heavenly city.

Yet even in my sadness I knew that God had given me an amazing gift. He had given me a hint of eternity, a moment of infinity, just a small foretaste of everlasting joy. I was able to see what few on earth get to see.

Even through my tears, I began praising God. I thanked him for this tiny moment of bliss, this fleeting glance at my everlasting home in heaven. I thanked him for his kindness and mercy and grace. And for everything he had given me – all the blessings and joy and meaning he had brought to my life. 'I know you're not finished with me yet, Lord,' I prayed. 'I understand. I'm excited to see you one day, but that will have to wait. Thank you for this wonderful vision. Thank you for being my Lord and Saviour.'

It was the sweetest brokenness I had ever known. Though my mind struggled to find the words to say, my heart was completely connected with God's. He took me to a special place where only a father and son can go.

Though I didn't fully understand it at the time, he was giving me courage for the days to come.

CHAPTER 19

As Long as the Heart Beats

God is not finished with you yet!

Dr David Greenberg and I have an interesting history. He's been my good friend and cardiologist for years, but in a way our relationship began long before we ever met. We discovered this truth by accident one day while talking in his office. The story goes like this.

Back in the days when I was warlord for the Mau Mau gang in New York, there was an old brick building in the centre of our neighbourhood. It was called Brooklyn Tech, and most of the students were white, middle-class kids. These young people were an easy target for harassment, and some of them probably had wallets full of cash on them, yet for some reason we left them completely alone. We never bothered them. We decided to let them come and go as they pleased.

More than that, we started protecting them from the other gangs around the neighbourhood. When we saw one of the students heading towards the school, we would watch them from a distance, just to make sure no one bothered them. If another street thug or gang member tried to approach them, we would quickly come to their aid. Protecting the students of this school became a personal project among our gang members. There was no rhyme or reason behind our actions; it was just something we decided to do.

David Greenberg was one of those students – just a young man pursuing his education in hopes of one day becoming a physician. And he was there during the years when I was running amok in the streets. He remembers well the protection he received from the Mau Maus while attending this school in one of the most dangerous sections of Brooklyn. Like the other students, he always wondered why this gang of street hoodlums would let them come and go without harm, even coming to their defence at the first sign of trouble. The students gladly accepted our help, but they never understood it. We didn't understand it either.

He and I never met formally until he became my physician many years later. But we can now both look back and see how God worked to protect him from harm so he could someday help many people, including me.

'I used to take care of you, and now it's your job to take care of me,' I joked with him once. Yet somehow we both knew it was more than a joke between friends. It was another confirmation of God's intervention in our lives.

The Test Results

This history with Dr Greenberg was on my mind while I sat in a procedure room, waiting to hear the results of the angiogram and other follow-up tests for my heart problem. Gloria was sitting and praying in a waiting room not far away.

I knew the minute Dr Greenberg walked into the room that the news wasn't good. 'Nicky,' he said, 'we found a problem with your tests.'

My throat sank into my stomach as he continued.

'It seems that several of the arteries on the left side of your chest have become constricted, causing a small section of your heart to be cut off from blood flow. I'm not sure how long this has been going on, but a piece of your heart appears to be dormant. We won't know how extensive the damage is, but that section of your heart tissue has died, leaving permanent damage.'

I didn't understand much of what he was saying. All I heard was that a piece of my heart was dormant or had died, and that seemed serious enough.

That very day, a medical team inserted stents into several of my blocked arteries. I certainly didn't enjoy having an operation, even one they called 'routine'. But I did enjoy getting to meet several of the staff and patients and to minister to many of them. And everything seemed to be going well with my recovery ... at least at first.

All I can say is, it's a good thing they don't let patients go home too soon, because later that afternoon I suffered several complications. My wife and daughter were in my room with me when I became weak and began to lose colour from my face. My daughter quickly got the nurse, and the medical team began to work on me with urgency.

Patrick called my office, and soon people across the country were praying for my health. It was a scary time for my family, but God took care of me through the entire evening.

The next morning Dr Greenberg let me leave the hospital, but only if I promised to take it as easy as possible over the coming days and weeks. He scheduled me for another visit in the coming weeks for more tests.

Back to the Doctor

Several times during the following week, Gloria would say to me, 'Nicky, aren't you worried? You need to slow down. You're not taking this seriously.'

The truth is, I wasn't worried. I knew that God would not let anything happen to me. 'I'm fine,' I would tell her.

In my spirit, after getting over the initial shock of my diagnosis and procedure, I was completely calm. I didn't know how God planned to take care of me, but I knew that he would. He had promised that nothing was going to happen to me, and I believed that promise. He was not finished with me yet.

During the weeks leading up to my appointment, I continued to hear from people who were praying for my health. It was encouraging to know how many people cared for me. And at every opportunity I assured them that I would be fine.

The day of my follow-up appointment with Dr Greenberg finally came, and once again I lay on the bed in the exam room while the technician examined my heart. At one point Gloria placed her finger over a part of my heart on the video screen and asked the technician, 'Did you check this area? That's where the problem is. Can you check to see if the damage has gotten any worse?'

She did a few more stabs and adjustments with the probe and then silently left the room. After that we waited for what seemed an eternity.

Finally Dr Greenberg walked into the room, his face beaming with excitement. He had been serious and sombre with me over the last few weeks, but now all that had changed.

'Nicky,' he said, 'I have some great news. I don't know how this happened, but it looks like the blood is flowing through that area of your heart again!'

Gloria said, 'Are you sure? It was supposed to be dormant.'

'I'm sure,' he answered. He repeated that he had no idea how this could have happened, but he assured us that the recent tests confirmed that my heart was somehow healed.

I'd seen God defeat the devil's plans so often by performing a miracle – and now he'd gone and done the same thing for me!

Gloria was thrilled at this turn of events, but she wasn't entirely surprised. I wasn't surprised at all. We both sensed that God would reach in and heal my heart, since he'd given advance assurance. But it was still a welcome miracle!

Living in God's Goodness

During my stay at the hospital, and indeed throughout my entire health scare, I used every opportunity to tell people about God's grace and mercy. I told anyone who would listen about my Lord and Saviour. Every nurse who came into the room got a message about Jesus. Several patients heard that I was there, so they came down to meet me, just to say hi. A couple even brought copies of my books for me to sign. Others were asking for books, so I sent Patrick to our office for them. Each time, I laughed with the people and prayed with them. I prayed for healing with the patients. I prayed for the doctors and nurses and house-keepers – anyone I could think of. An evangelist is an evangelist all the time.

While I was sitting in the exam room, waiting to leave, Dr Greenberg said to me, 'Nicky, look what you've done to this place. Everyone is smiling and laughing. Everyone is talking about you!'

'No, Dr Greenberg,' I said. 'You've got it wrong. They're not talking about me; they're talking about the One who lives inside of me! They're talking about Jesus! I just say what he tells me to say. It's he who has made them all so happy. He's the one who has brought joy to this place!'

Dr Greenberg is a beautiful Jewish man, and I deeply appreciate him and his lovely wife. They do a lot for our community. I look forward to attending synagogue with them someday soon, as I have promised him.

Life is filled with opportunities to spread God's good-ness. Every moment is another chance to hurt the enemy and display God's love – both at the same time. Every day brings new opportunities for enlarging the kingdom of heaven.

This is what spiritual warfare is all about. It's not about sitting in your room with a scowl on your face, buffeting your body and claiming dominion over temptation. It's not about wandering the neighbourhood with holy water, trying to bind the enemy. It's about living each and every moment in the grace and mercy of God. It's about letting the Spirit move you where you can do the most good. Most of all, it's about telling others of God's marvellous love and grace. He's the only one who can bring fulfilment to your life.

This is where the real battle is fought. This is where the supernatural war for souls is being played out. This is how you beat back the devil!

Soldiering On

I don't have a prophetic word for you, like those seven people had for me as I narrated in the previous chapter. I can't tell you for sure that you're going to have much more time on this earth. But most likely it's true. Most likely God is not finished with you here just yet.

And so, just like me, you need not fear. You can say with the apostle Paul, 'The Lord will rescue me from every evil attack and will bring me safely to his heavenly kingdom.'[1] Or take heart in the words of John: 'The one who was born of God keeps him safe, and the evil one cannot harm him.'[2]

God is ready to preserve your life. He's ready to do miracles, if needed, to keep you in his service. He still wants you to fight on his side.

You may be weary in struggling against the enemy. If so, I understand that. Temptation, affliction, distractions, deception, outright attacks – these all take their toll. But as the Scriptures say, 'Let us not become weary in doing good.'[3]

If I, after all I've been through, still have some fight in me, then I bet you do too! In fact, I'll go further than that. I believe that you're not just going to keep on fighting. I believe that your greatest time of victories for the Lord may yet lie ahead of you. He's eager to perform signs and wonders in and all around you to push back the devil's influence and establish the kingdom of his wonderful Son.

I pray that he will do that in your life. And I pray that you'll say, 'Yes, Lord!'

Eventually, of course, there will come a time to lay down our swords and cease our battle with the devil. There will come a time for us to leave this life. And when that time comes, we can have full confidence of remaining in God's care every moment. One day we'll push the button and the doors of heaven will open. And. The. Sight. Will. Be. Glorious!

Near to God

The devil has no mother. He's a hopeless case, unredeemable. As long as he's free, he'll never stop seeking to steal, kill and destroy. He's worse than we've been accustomed to thinking, and it's long since time we recognised that.

BUT

God is greater than we could ever think! He's Almighty, never for one moment fearing what the devil can do. He has a plan for victory, and step by step he is working it out in history through the sacrifice of his Son and – believe it or not – with the help of the likes of us. If we need to recognise that the devil is alive and active in the world, that goes double for recognising what God is doing. He is working astounding miracles every day to establish his kingdom of glory.

Let's recall what we've learned about him in recent chapters.

Chapter 13:

The devil is a defeated foe because of Christ. In our day God is doing mighty works that turn back the works of the devil.

Chapter 14:

We can live out the book of Acts, for God is ready to do signs and wonders that overturn the dominion of darkness and establish his kingdom of light.

Chapter 15:

Every person on this planet has a miracle in their life that God is waiting to perform. He will display his power in his time for each one of us.

Chapter 16:

We must have simple, bold faith in God. And as we do, we will see a massive outpouring of God's power to establish his great works.

Chapter 17:

Whenever we exercise our God-given authority in prayer, the downtrodden are raised up and Satan falls from his lofty place all over again. This kind of warfare praying is something every believer can do.

Chapters 18 and 19:

God is not finished with us yet. As we renounce the devil and cooperate with the King, the best is still to come!

A part of warfare is having an effective defence. But the better part – the part that secures the final victory – is having a bold offence. The apostle James, after saying, 'Resist the devil, and he will flee from you,' said with his next breath, 'Come near to God and he will come near to you.'[4] That's what we must do. Come near to our almighty God in faith, in holiness, in boldness. For victory lies with him.

PART 4

Our Spiritual Warfare

Be strong in the Lord and in his mighty power. Put on the full armour of God so that you can take your stand against the devil's schemes.

(Ephesians 6:10–11)

CHAPTER 20

The Arsenal

Weapons for spiritual warfare

When Lucifer fell from heaven and came to inhabit the earth with his demons, the spiritual war that had begun above broke out again here below. As we have seen, it isn't the kind of war that's easily observable, like armies marching or missiles flying. It began with a serpent hissing lies to a woman in a garden in order to get her to do what she wasn't supposed to: eat forbidden fruit. And the spiritual warfare has continued throughout the generations ever since then with temptation, insinuation, accusation, deception, scare tactics and sometimes more obvious assaults. These are the devil's weapons.

But we have weapons too. Spiritual weapons. Divine weapons. With them, we 'fight the good fight' and each of us is enabled to serve as 'a good soldier of Christ Jesus'.[1] We fight on the side of truth in the battlefield of our minds and the battlefield of the world all around us.

For though we live in the world, we do not wage war as the world does. The weapons we fight with are not the weapons of the world. On the contrary, they have divine power to demolish strongholds. We demolish arguments and every pretension that sets itself up against the knowledge of God, and we take captive every thought to make it obedient to Christ.[2]

As I've said before, there are no non-combatants. We have to fight, whether we want to or not. And since that's the case, we'd better learn to use the weapons God gives us. That's what this chapter is all about. Here we bring together all we have learned about how to fight in the spiritual war that's underway.

Consider this chapter the arsenal for soldiers of the Lord. Pick up your weapons and learn to fight.

The Armour of God

Scripture mentions many ways to walk in strength and victory, and we don't have the space to look at all of them. But any discussion of how to overcome Satan's ploys should begin with the armour of God that Paul described in Ephesians 6:

Be strong in the Lord and in his mighty power. Put on the full armour of God so that you can take your stand against the devil's schemes. For our struggle is not against flesh and blood, but against the rulers, against the authorities, against the powers of this dark world and against the spiritual forces of evil in the heavenly realms. Therefore put on the full armour of God, so that when the day of evil comes, you may be able to stand your ground, and after you have done everything, to stand. Stand firm then, with the belt of truth buckled round your waist, with the breastplate of righteousness in place, and with your feet fitted with the readiness that comes from the gospel of peace. In addition to all this, take up the shield of faith, with which you can extinguish all the flaming arrows of the evil one. Take the helmet of salvation and the sword of the Spirit, which is the word of God. And pray in the Spirit on all occasions with all kinds of prayers and requests. With this in mind, be alert and always keep on praying for all the saints.[3]

Our loving heavenly Father has spelled out precisely how to defeat our adversary in this precious section of his Word – truth, righteousness, the gospel, faith, salvation, praying in the Spirit. His Word tells us exactly how to overcome, and his Spirit will give us the power to do just that. Take the time to study these truths, and ask God for strength to make them a reality in your life.

Meanwhile, I want to emphasise a few of the weapons listed in Ephesians 6, along with a few others we know about from elsewhere in Scripture.

A Shield against the Devil's Arrows: Faith

Faith in Christ is the bedrock of our entire relationship with God. But it not only seals our eternal destiny; faith is also repeatedly described in the Bible as a powerful force that allows us to be victorious in our Christian lives.

When Paul talked about the armour of God, one of the weapons he mentioned is faith. Paul called it a shield and said that, with faith, we can put out the flaming arrows that Satan hurls at us. Peter, too, told the Church that we are shielded by God's power through faith.[4] What a promise! We know that Satan's arrows will come, but when we have the shield of faith, they can't hurt us. Clearly, faith is not optional – we must see that it defines our very lives. And faith that has not been tested cannot be trusted.

I've spent over half a century – well over half my life – trying to build up the kingdom of God and tear down the kingdom of Satan. And I've seen so many victories. The stories I tell in this book are only a tiny fraction of what I could share. These experiences have built my faith in the power of God to overcome evil. I pray that over the course of your life God will show you many faith-building evidences of his supreme power.

The Way to Be Powerful and Effective: Fervent Prayer

On the night when Jesus was wrestling in prayer with his mission to die on the cross, his disciples couldn't keep their eyes open, much less support him in prayer. So Jesus said to them, 'Watch and pray so that you will not fall into temptation. The spirit is willing, but the body is weak.'[5]

Prayer is a fundamental, indispensable weapon in our struggle against evil spiritual forces. In the book of James, we read that 'the prayer of a righteous man is powerful and effective'.[6] A simple prayer can rally the forces of heaven to protect us from harm. Through prayer we gain the strength and knowledge we need to overcome temptation, discern God's will or receive anything else we need. God gives supernatural wisdom and power to those who trust him, and he longs to do just that.

It's sad when believers see prayer as nothing more than the recitation of a wish list or a last-ditch call for help. So many people spend their prayer times begging God for things they want, asking him to fulfil their selfish desires. God doesn't promise to answer those kinds of prayers. But when we pray according to his will, and for what we truly need in advancing the kingdom, he answers.

When we move in God's will, we can depend on him to open doors for us – to make a path and guide us as we go along. We can feel his constant presence as we go about our daily tasks. I've experienced this so many times in my life and ministry. I could list endless personal examples – financial attacks on our ministry, my granddaughter's sickness, and so much more. But I always believe his word that he'll never leave me alone or forsake my simple faith.

Fervent prayer is a lifestyle of going to God with every need and concern and question, then learning to obey when we sense him answering. It is petitioning God for direction before we move and then going in the direction where we see him pointing. I'm convinced that if we do that, if we live our lives in earnest prayer and a commitment to obedience, if we honestly seek God's wisdom and try to move in the direction he leads, then even if we go the wrong way from time to time, God will eventually make it right.

In Chapter 17 I pointed out Norman Roman's mother as an example of a prayer warrior who was bringing God's power to bear behind the scenes before God did something miraculous. But let me tell you this: in every story I've told where God defeated the devil, *somebody* was praying. David Wilkerson prayed for me. I prayed for my parents. My whole family prayed for my nephew Tato. And so on it goes.

We must pray. Pray boldly. Pray believing. And God will do the rest.

The Environment that Nurtures Victory: Worship

Was it a coincidence that God decided to rescue Paul and Silas from prison in Philippi just when they were praying and singing hymns?[7] I don't think so! I believe God wanted to show them that he heard and honoured their worship of him. And he'll break our bonds too when we worship him.

If you'll recall from Chapter 10, when a demon began to manifest itself in a man at a California church, I asked the congregation to keep up a flow of worship. That wasn't just to keep them busy while a team of us were working to cast out the demon. The congregation's worship was a crucial part of the casting out.

You see, Lucifer hates the worship of God. He wants to receive worship himself. That's why he rebelled against God in the first place – to take God's place. So when we worship God, we are creating an environment that's toxic to the devil and his demons. We should never underestimate the power of worship.

214

There are many forms of worship that we can lift up to God, and all of them make us stronger in our faith and insulate us from the enemy of our souls. Also, any time that we acknowledge God as our Lord and Saviour, we are bringing a critical level of perspective into our lives. We are acknowledging that he is God and we are not. We are reminding ourselves of his lordship over the universe and our lives.

Worship can be as simple as acknowledging God's goodness and power in our hearts during prayer. Or it can be a time of brokenness or unspeakable joy. Or it can be singing and praising out loud. Regardless, there is tremendous power in worship – power beyond what most of us might believe.

In the book of 2 Chronicles, we read that the army of Jehoshaphat, king of Judah, was about to be overpowered by a vastly stronger force coming against them. The king prayed to God, 'We do not know what to do, but our eyes are upon you.' The Spirit of the Lord told them not to be afraid, that the Lord would be with them. The very next day, 'Jehoshaphat appointed men to sing to the LORD and to praise him for the splendour of his holiness as they went out at the head of the army, saying: "Give thanks to the LORD, for his love endures forever."'

What happened next? 'As they began to sing and praise, the LORD set ambushes against the men of Ammon and Moab and Mount Seir who were invading Judah, and they were defeated.'[8]

What a powerful story! The next time you come up against what looks like insurmountable odds, begin praising God with all your might, and watch Satan run for cover.

The Sword of the Spirit: God's Word

In his description of the armour of God, Paul calls the Word of God 'the sword of the Spirit'.[9] The Bible, then, is not just a book; it is a living Word activated by the Holy Spirit. And it is a weapon to use in spiritual warfare. As the writer of Hebrews says, 'The word of God is living and active. Sharper than any double-edged sword, it penetrates even to dividing soul and spirit, joints and marrow; it judges the thoughts and attitudes of the heart.'[10]

The devil is the Father of lies, but the Holy Spirit is the 'Spirit of truth'.[11] And when he speaks the truth through the Scripture he has inspired, the deceptions of the devil are revealed.

Think about it. When Jesus himself was tempted by Satan, what weapon did he use? Scripture, of course. Every time the devil offered him something the Father did not intend for him, Jesus countered with a teaching from the Word that showed it would be wrong for him to take the bait.[12] And the devil had to retreat.

We, too, can use Scripture against the devil when we are tempted. For example, if someone is an alcoholic, he can memorise Ephesians 5:18: 'Do not get drunk on wine, which leads to debauchery [excessive indulgence in sensual pleasures]. Instead, be filled with the Spirit.' Then he can repeat it to himself whenever he is tempted to go back to the bottle. It is not a magic talisman. It is a way to bury the truth deep inside – and repel the devil.

There is no way to overstate the power of God's Word in the heart, mind and life of a believer. God works in mysterious ways when we hear or read his Word. When we take time to read and meditate on Scripture daily, a supernatural wisdom is imparted into us. When we speak it to the devil, he knows he is getting nowhere with us.

Beyond that, knowing Scripture can keep us from error. Those who are aware of the Bible's repeated condemnation of the occult should be less inclined to dabble in such practices. And as our culture drifts from its Judeo-Christian moorings, it becomes more and more important that we know and obey biblical teaching. It's the antidote to the devil's deceptions.

God spoke to every believer through his prophet Joshua when he said, 'Do not let this Book of the Law depart from your mouth; meditate on it day and night, so that you may be careful to do everything written in it. Then you will be prosperous and successful.'[13] Through study of Scripture, God will impart within us all the wisdom and strength we need to achieve his will for us. Our Christian walk *will* succeed if we obey this simple principle of obedience and faith.

Read Scripture. Meditate on it. And memorise it, especially verses about God's power and his victory over the devil. Start with the verses I have listed in the Appendix.

God's Army: Christian Community

I know of a man who runs a small Christian ministry who has made a curious choice: he has decided not to have a home church. His theology is pretty far outside the mainstream, and he says he's never found a church that he can agree with, so he just doesn't go. He spends his Sunday mornings on his back porch, reading a good book, sometimes preparing a sermon, convinced that he is doing God's will.

But he is wrong. Dead wrong. He is choosing to ignore a critical element of the Christian faith, not to mention a direct mandate from Scripture.[14] And in doing so, he is allowing his faith to grow stagnant and weak. When he speaks, he often cites his lifelong struggle with sin, and it's no wonder. By choosing to disregard God's command to fellowship with other believers, he is setting himself up for temptation, self-righteousness and false teaching.

There is a supernatural element to corporate times of fellowship. When we join and fellowship with a local body of believers, we are not only obeying Scripture, we are also allowing God to work in us through the encouragement and admonition of other Christians.

I can't count the number of times that God has spoken to me through a minister or a song or through other believers. When a group of Christians gather together, God uses the opportunity to build each one up individually. He moves through their midst, speaking and touching each one – often in a different way. That's the beauty of the family of Christ. Through fellowship, we find strength and power and discipline. Through meeting together, our faith grows.

And healthy fellowship is important outside of worship services as well. Each of us should find people of like mind and values – people who will not only commit to being our friend but also hold us accountable. People who will mentor us in our faith, help us resist temptation and pick us up when we fall. People who will be there to encourage us during times of stress and turmoil and admonish us when we are missing the boat. People who want to see us succeed in our Christian walk and whom we can encourage when they, too, face difficulties.

Whenever my organisation holds an evangelistic outreach, we always try to partner with local Christian churches and ministries. We know that our efforts will be more successful, and our influence longer lasting, if we are tied in with other believers who are praying, evangelising and discipling for the Lord.

Do you remember that time when gay rights activists were trying to shut our crusade down in the UK (Chapter 11)? I don't know what we would have done without the support of Christians in England and all over Europe. They forced the officials who were opposing us to let us go on with our preaching unhindered. Thank God for the Christian community!

Conclusion

Our enemy is a fearsome one. *Ese hombre no tiene madre.* By now you know this, even if you didn't before. You're no longer like so many Christians of our day, living as if they are ignorant of the devil. You also know that our God is much more powerful than the devil can ever be. You cannot compare the created with the Creator! Time and time again he wins, and in the end he will put the devil away forever.

As our Commander-in-Chief, God does not leave us defenceless against our enemy. He gives us weapons forged and tempered to bring his power to bear in the struggles we find ourselves in. We pray fervently. Worship with all our hearts. Remain in fellowship with other believers. Step out in faith, trusting God to lead. Examine the Scriptures daily. And put on the full armour of God in order to overcome the enemy. With these weapons, we are prepared and in control.

We need not fear that the devil will shake us. *We* can shake *him*! What I've learned is that the devil is stupid. He always gets caught! That's because he gives us clues that show us how to fight him. Our weapons are perfectly suited to parrying his attacks and sending him into retreat.

The demons tremble at God's presence. They tremble at ours, too, when we are determined and are using the weapons God gives us. As we submit to God and resist the devil, he must flee.[15]

Fellow soldier, let us not fear the spiritual war. Let us not even hesitate. We've got the commission from God – authority over the enemy. We are more than conquerors!

CHAPTER 21

The Church Victorious

A call for a new movement

For thousands of years, Lucifer poured out his hate on the new creation of God, those humans down on earth. It was great sport. He and his demons got dark enjoyment out of every victory over their victims. Out of every sickness inflicted. Every temptation accepted. Every act of violence or abuse or rejection. Every death.

But all the time, Lucifer remembered what God had said to him in the Garden of Eden after he had begun his campaign by assuming the form of a serpent to tempt Eve. 'I will put enmity between you and the woman,' cursed God, 'and between your offspring and hers; he will crush your head, and you will strike his heel.'

Lucifer's head crushed! The great and powerful Lucifer, created as the mightiest of the angels! It could not be that he would be defeated by one of the offspring of the human race. Yes, God said that he would return injury – 'strike his heel'. But that didn't sound anything like being crushed!

The thought of this predicted defeat never left his mind. And then there was the frustration over the limitation of what he could accomplish. Over the years, he would trick, mutilate and frighten whenever he could, but God would let him affect people only so far and no farther.

There was the time he managed to get the human race almost to the point where he wanted it. 'Every inclination of the thoughts of man's heart was only evil all the time.' That's what Lucifer liked to see! But then what did God do? He eliminated the wicked people with a flood and started the human race over again with the one righteous man who was left – Noah. How enraging for Lucifer!

But Lucifer bided his time. What else could he do? Besides, he knew that he could keep working on those weak, sinful humans. After some time, things were looking better for him. The human race, having spread across the earth, was practising all kinds of religions that didn't honour God. But then God intervened again. This time he created a nation out of another righteous man, Abraham – a nation that would embody God's hope for the human race and receive his law.

Again Lucifer had to go back to work. Generation after generation, he did everything he could to pull the chosen nation back in his direction. There would be periodic God-honouring revivals, but Lucifer knew that he was winning – the nation was spiralling ever downward into disobedience. It was delicious. But at last the prediction Lucifer had tried to forget went into effect.

A woman of the human race had a very special Child.

Defeat snatched from the jaws of victory

Lucifer knew he had trouble on his hands. Out of the chosen nation that he had managed to spiritually neutralise so many times had come a man like no other. A man who was also God! This could bode no good for Lucifer.

As soon as Jesus began his ministry, Lucifer went to work on him. Unlike Eve, Jesus wasn't in a garden; he was in a desert at the time. But otherwise it was much the same. The devil showed up and offered him choices that would have derailed his mission. Lucifer didn't come out and say it, but what he meant was this: 'Don't be obedient and provide the sacrifice that the Father asks for; seize high position now, under me, the prince of the earth!' A powerful incentive. But it didn't work. Jesus was no pushover like Eve.

From then on, things really got bad for Lucifer. Jesus sent Lucifer's minions running in terror whenever he encountered them. And what was worse, he gave the same authority over the demons to his followers. It was maddening. When these followers went out and defeated his plans, it felt to Lucifer like he was being cast down from heaven all over again.

But then came Lucifer's big chance. Always loving to kill and destroy, Lucifer now had the opportunity to do just that to the Son of God. The Father turned his back on the Son, who had become the sin offering for the world, and the devil had a free hand to make the Son suffer and die. When the Son breathed his last, it felt so good to the devil.

He thought he had won! But he had only struck the heel of this Man.

Lucifer's own head was crushed when three days later Jesus came back to life. He had slipped out of Lucifer's grasp – forever. This was the bitterest blow to Lucifer. 'Having disarmed the powers and authorities, Jesus made a public spectacle of them, triumphing over them by the cross.'

Lucifer knew something had changed drastically. He was still free and active in the world, but now his doom was certain. Time and again people were rescued from Lucifer's 'dominion of darkness' and brought into 'the kingdom of the Son'. It was enough to make the devil gnash his already well-gnashed teeth.

His best hope was to convince Jesus' followers to overlook him or minimise his awfulness. If they didn't know how dangerous he was, they would forget their authority over him, given to them by God. So that's what he did. And meanwhile, he and his devils, knowing that their time was limited, began working more frantically than ever to pull as many people down with them as possible.[1]

Final Destination: Lake of Fire

One day a time will come when Lucifer will copy God's strategy. He'll choose to work through one man. Not the Christ but the Anti-Christ. This will be Lucifer's great hope to regain control over the world. No one knows when or exactly how this will happen. But it will involve Lucifer's greatest feat of pulling a cloak of deception over the human race. And it will nearly succeed.

We can see those awful days only as in a haze, scenes and images appearing in the swirling mist. Death riding on a pale horse, with Hades following behind. The sun turning black, the moon turning blood red, the stars falling from the sky. A third of the earth burning up. Cries of 'Woe!' Massed armies. Spreading plagues. Bloodshed and death on an unprecedented scale.

The warfare will be like the previous warfare in heaven when Lucifer was first cast down, but it will be even worse. And this time the Lord's champion will not be the archangel Michael. It will be the Lamb who was slain. It will be the Lion of the tribe of Judah. The rider on the white horse who defeats the devil and his wicked human representative will be Christ himself. Under him, the victory will be complete.

One who got a fore-glimpse of the punishment handed out to the devil described it as a thousand-year jail sentence:

> I saw an angel coming down out of heaven, having the key to the Abyss and holding in his hand a great chain. He seized the dragon, that ancient serpent, who is the devil, or Satan, and bound him for a thousand years. He threw him into the Abyss, and locked and sealed it over him, to keep him from deceiving the nations any more until the thousand years were ended. After that, he must be set free for a short time.[2]

The thousand years when the earth is free of the devil will be a time like no other. Imagine what it would be like to have the evil one locked up, gone – how wonderful! It's a state we can only dream about now. And it will happen. But then there will be one last outbreak of violence before the devil is finally lost sight of.

> When the thousand years are over, Satan will be released from his prison and will go out to deceive the nations in the four corners of the earth – Gog and Magog – to gather them for battle. In number they are like the sand on the seashore. They marched across the breadth of the earth and surrounded the camp of God's people, the city he loves. But fire came down from heaven and devoured them. And the devil, who deceived them, was thrown into the lake of burning sulphur, where the beast and the false prophet had been thrown. They will be tormented day and night for ever and ever.[3]

This is 'the eternal fire prepared for the devil and his angels', the place where, deep down, Lucifer knows even now that he is headed. None of us need waste a minute of our time mourning his fate. He has earned every bit of the eternity he will spend in hell. Good riddance to the motherless one!

The Church Stymied

What's saddest to me is the fate of the people Satan is successful with on earth. Those he manages to permanently blind to the love of God will never have their names written in the book of life. If they follow the devil, they will end up with him in the lake of fire.[4]

And then there are all the other ways that Satan causes harm. All the sin, the sickness, the frustration. I don't need to go into it any more; hopefully, through this book I have already made it plain. Frankly, I'm tired of writing about the devil. Enough!

My point is that the final defeat of the devil, the completion of the work Christ began on the cross, is still in the future tense. That's *tomorrow*. *Today* we must fight.

And are we being successful? How is the worldwide Body of Christ doing at establishing the kingdom of God today?

Here's what I see. We have churches and conferences and organisations galore, but we're all too often preaching a watered-down gospel, not the essential truths about sin and salvation. Churches and denominations are competing against one another instead of working together to defeat our common foe, the devil. As we've grown, we may have become powerful in a worldly sense, but at the same time we're limiting the true power of God because we're not acting with his authority. We're not using the keys of the kingdom that God entrusted to us. We're binding nothing and loosing nothing.

Let me share with you some statistics I have recently discovered about pastors. I trust they will sober you as much as they do me.

- 50 per cent of pastors' marriages now end in divorce.
- 80 per cent of pastors feel unqualified and therefore discouraged.
- 84 per cent of their spouses feel unqualified and therefore discouraged.

- 50 per cent of pastors say they would resign if they were qualified to do anything else.
- 80 per cent of new seminary graduates will quit the ministry within the first five years.
- 70 per cent of pastors fight constant depression.
- 40 per cent of pastors admit to having an affair since the beginning of their ministry.

If this is what the experience of our church leaders is like, is it any wonder that Christians in general are filled with apathy, feeling as if the Church has somehow gone astray?

The devil, instead of fleeing from us, must be laughing at us from the shadows right now.

Now, let me assure you that I love the Church. After all, I am a part of the Church, the Body of Christ. I don't despise the Church. Entirely the opposite. I travel all the time to work with churches and ministries in outreaches all over the world. And it is because I love the Church that I must be honest and tell what I have seen. Some churches, just like some individuals, are serving God faithfully. But far too many churches are just going through the motions, making little impact. And this is why the tide of the spiritual war is running against us, despite the future victory the Bible has told us to expect.

If it's any consolation, the kind of apathy we see today is hardly original to us.

Climbing Back to the Heights

The first-century church of Ephesus was blessed like few others. The apostle Paul spent a couple of years there, making it his base of ministry operations. Later he wrote a letter to the church, one which now appears in the Bible. It is believed that the apostle John also lived there, possibly bringing Mary the mother of Jesus to live near him in her elderly years. For decades the church was an effective centre of the new Christian faith, birthing several daughter churches in the surrounding area. The Ephesian believers had one common sense of direction – to go after the community together for Christ.

So, near the end of the first century, why did Christ say to the church of Ephesus, 'I hold this against you: You have forsaken your first love'?[5] Although they were still doing some good things, somehow they had become complacent. They had lost their passion for God. Once they were filled with faith and zeal, ready to build up the kingdom of God on the devil's own ground at any cost to themselves, but now they were satisfied with routine and comfort and the status quo.

My friends, the church of Ephesus is us! *We* have lost our first love for God. How else can we explain our indifference to the works of the devil? What else would account for our failure to not only *believe* that God can do miracles but also *expect* him to do them before our very eyes?

So, what are we to do? The answer lies in Christ's call to the church of Ephesus: 'Remember the height from which you have fallen!' Isn't that an interesting image? Just as the devil fell from the heights of heaven, so we fall from the heights when we aren't passionate about God anymore. But Jesus goes on to explain what he means: 'Repent and do the things you did at first.' And with it comes a warning, because Christ would not have us be ignorant of what is at stake: 'If you do not repent, I will come to you and remove your lampstand from its place.'[6]

In my evangelistic crusades, I always end with an altar call. I invite people to come to the front and confess their sins to God, because confession releases pent-up spiritual suffering and breaks the hold that the devil has on them, removing shame, guilt and fear. After their confession, the Spirit can fill them and they can go on in God's power and love.

Right now I am issuing an altar call for the whole Church. It's not that every member of the Church has failed to recognise the devil's wickedness or live in God's power. But as a whole, the Church has more and more failed in this area. Collectively, we need to confess our sin and start again with God. Let us repent of our failure to love God and hate the devil. Let us empty ourselves in humility so that God can fill us with his Spirit of power to be victorious.

The devil's only going lower: he's already fallen from heaven, and he's headed towards the Abyss. But by God's grace we can climb back to the heights from which we have fallen. We can get back to an intimacy of relationship with God. We can get back to our first love, Jesus.

And when we do, it will change *everything*.

Jesus People II

From time to time, history has shown us that the Church can go through a powerful revival in which she recaptures God's vision for her. These revivals carry names like the Reformation and the Great Awakening. Another revival happened in my lifetime, and it's usually called the Jesus People Movement. I remember it vividly.

The teenage gang problem of which I was a part in the late 1950s was, in a way, a precursor of where the entire youth of America would go in the 1960s and early 1970s. So many older people in those years were worried – with good reason – about the younger generation because of drug use, casual sex, resistance to authority and other dangerous behaviours. But God stepped in and created a revival that rescued untold thousands of these young people. They joined the Jesus People Movement and brought new life to the Church. I saw it firsthand when I was working with Teen Challenge and then as I travelled about the nation and the world as an evangelist.

Flash forward to the opening decades of the twenty-first century. Here is what I sense: we need another movement of God in our day. We need another revival. Jesus People II, we might call it, because it has to be all about Jesus.

Like any movement from God, it will involve moving ahead by getting back to what's really important. Getting back to prayer. Getting back to loving one another. Getting back to preaching the gospel in all boldness. Getting back to helping the needy. Most of all, getting back to Jesus, the one who defeated the devil, who brought us into his kingdom and who gave us his authority to use.

With this kind of renewal, the Church will be transformed. No longer will churches be competitive organisations, striving to build up their own little kingdoms. Instead, they will be turned into Holy Ghost hospitals, offering God's healing for the world's ills of hopelessness, loneliness, sin and so much more of the devil's traps. Church members will go out from their four walls and meet needs around them. They won't just pray; they'll also act. Even small churches will understand that God will do great things through them. And whereas now we are losing our youth in the inner cities and in the suburbs, youth will become excited as they begin to see the Church's God-given mission as a cause worth giving their lives to. As a matter of fact, I believe youth will drive Jesus People II just as they did Jesus People I.

You may not think you could ever be a part of such a work of God. It seems impossible, given where you're at right now. You may be in financial difficulties, in sickness, having many needs, going through many hardships and loneliness. But the Lord has not left you, nor will he ever leave you. Never!

With a renewed understanding of the awful wickedness of the devil and the awesome greatness of our God, we will turn the tide of spiritual warfare. We will see those miracles of God of which I've spoken – and greater miracles still. It will be none of our own doing; it will all be of Christ. His is the power that brings the victory. So there's no room for the devil's vice of pride. Only worship of the Worthy One.

This is what the devil fears, for it hastens the building of the kingdom of God. It hastens the return of Christ. It hastens the devil's own doom.

Let me say it again: it's time for a new movement in the Church.

It's time for waking up to the danger posed by the devil, the motherless evildoer.

And even more, it's time for waking up to the power of God and all he wants to do in us, through us and around us.

This is the generation. Now is the time.

Let it begin with us.

Over the years of my Christian life, I've tried to be faithful to my God and my calling, and I pray that you will do the same. And that you will join with me and the many other voices rising up in the name of God, proclaiming a powerful message against the evil one. Let us rise up together and proclaim that, in the mighty name of Jesus, we will not relent. We will not give up. We will stand strong with our Lord and Saviour until our very last breath!

Perhaps one day it will be said of us what the book of Revelation says of another group of spiritual warriors:

Now have come the salvation and the power
    and the kingdom of our God,
    and the authority of his Christ.
For the accuser of our brothers,
    who accuses them before our God day and night,
    has been hurled down.

They overcame him
　　by the blood of the Lamb
　　and by the word of their testimony;
they did not love their lives so much
　　as to shrink from death.
Therefore rejoice, you heavens
　　and you who dwell in them![7]

Amen.

Acknowledgements

First, to my wife of more than fifty years, Gloria Cruz. Her constant advice and prayer, along with her intimate knowledge of Scripture, were priceless assets to this project. Years ago, I promised Gloria that I would never write another book on Satan and the dark world. But a few years ago we felt that it was urgent to address this critical subject one more time. In doing so, my family and my staff have paid the price, as it seemed at times that all hell was unleashed against us to stop this project through physical attacks and intimidation.

A special heartfelt thanks to Eric and Elisa Stanford from Edit Resource (www.editresource.com), who helped push this book through to its completion. I had been working on the book for four years. At times I wondered if it would ever see the light of day. Eric, thank you for bringing in fresh perspective and insight.

I want to thank my personal assistant of over ten years, Karen Robinson, who invested countless hours working with me and my editor. She must have been frustrated with so many changes and rewrites over the past forty-eight months. Still, she kept pressing forward to make sure everything stayed on track. Her advice and input were invaluable.

Patrick, our CEO here at Nicky Cruz Outreach for more than twenty years, was a tremendous help with his knowledge and education. He carefully went through and corrected the manuscript many times. His input on the Greek and Hebrew and insight into the Scriptures inspired me. I want to thank him for going through the manuscript page by page through seemingly endless hours and with the loss of much sleep. He is my son-in-law, but I should call him my son-in-love! I am forever grateful for his help.

Appendix:

Spiritual Warfare Memory Verses

Matthew 6:13: 'Lead us not into temptation, but deliver us from the evil one.'

Matthew 16:18: 'I will build my church, and the gates of Hades will not overcome it.'

John 10:10: 'The thief comes only to steal and kill and destroy; I have come that they may have life, and have it to the full.'

John 12:31: 'Now is the time for judgment on this world; now the prince of this world will be driven out.'

Romans 8:37: 'We are more than conquerors through him who loved us.'

Romans 12:21: 'Do not be overcome by evil, but overcome evil with good.'

Romans 16:20: 'The God of peace will soon crush Satan under your feet.'

2 Corinthians 10:4: 'The weapons we fight with are not the weapons of the world. On the contrary, they have divine power to demolish strongholds.'

Ephesians 6:10–11: 'Be strong in the Lord and in his mighty power. Put on the full armour of God so that you can take your stand against the devil's schemes.'

Colossians 1:13: 'He has rescued us from the dominion of darkness and brought us into the kingdom of the Son he loves.'

2 Thessalonians 3:3: 'The Lord is faithful, and he will strengthen and protect you from the evil one.'

1 Timothy 6:12: 'Fight the good fight of the faith.'

2 Timothy 4:18: 'The Lord will rescue me from every evil attack and will bring me safely to his heavenly kingdom.'

James 4:7–8: 'Resist the devil, and he will flee from you. Come near to God and he will come near to you.'

1 John 4:4: 'The one who is in you is greater than the one who is in the world.'

1 John 5:18: 'The one who was born of God keeps him safe, and the evil one cannot harm him.'

Notes

Chapter 1

1 Ephesians 6:12.
2 2 Corinthians 2:11.

Chapter 2

1 The majority of our information about the devil's career comes from Isaiah 14:12–15, Ezekiel 28:11–19, Revelation 12 and Revelation 20:1–3, 7–10. The story above includes word-for-word quotations from Isaiah 14:13–14 and Revelation 12:12.
2 2 Corinthians 4:4; John 14:30; 1 John 5:19; John 8:44; Revelation 12:9; Revelation 12:10; Ephesians 2:2; 1 Peter 5:8; Revelation 12:9; John 10:10.
3 Mark 5:9; Revelation 12:4.
4 Revelation 20:10.
5 Romans 16:20; James 4:7.
6 Luke 11:21–22.
7 Matthew 28:18.
8 Matthew 10:1; Luke 10:18–19. Compare disputed verse Mark 16:17.
9 Matthew 16:17–19; 18:18.
10 Matthew 10:16, ESV; Revelation 20:2.

Chapter 3

1   Hebrews 1:3.
2   Mark 3:29.
3   John 15:18–19.
4   Ephesians 5:15–16.
5   Genesis 3:1 – 4:16.
6   Matthew 6:13.
7   Romans 8:37–39.

Chapter 4

1   1 Samuel 28.
2   Leviticus 20:6; Galatians 5:20.
3   Proverbs 4:23, KJV.
4   John 8:44.
5   2 Corinthians 4:4.
6   Isaiah 8:19–20.

Chapter 6

1   1 John 5:18.
2   James 4:7.
3   Jude 8–10.
4   Revelation 12:11.

Chapter 7

1   2 Corinthians 11:14.
2   Isaiah 5:20.

Chapter 8

1 Hebrews 4:12–13.
2 1 Samuel 16:14; 18:9–11; 19:9; Mark 7:32–33; Matthew 12:22; Mark 1:26; 9:17, 20, 22, 25; Luke 13:11.
3 2 Corinthians 12:7.
4 Job 2:7; see all of Job 1 and 2.

Chapter 9

1 Colossians 1:13.
2 Exodus 20:5.

Chapter 10

1 Judges 9:23–24; 1 Samuel 16:14–23; 18:10–11; 19:9–10; 1 Chronicles 21:1; Zechariah 3:1–2; Matthew 4:23–24; 8:16–17, 28–34; 9:32–34; 10:1; 12:22–32, 43–45; 13: 37–39; 15:22–28; 17:14–21; Mark 1:23–27; 3:11–12; 5:1–20; 6:7; 7:25–30; 8:33; 9:14–29, 38–40; 16:9, 17; Luke 4:33–36, 41; 8:1–3, 26–39; 9:37–42, 49; 10:17–20; 11:14–26; John 13:27; Acts 5:3, 16; 8:7; 16:16–18; 19:11–16; 1 Corinthians 10:21; 2 Corinthians 12:7.
2 Mark 5:1–20.
3 Genesis 3.
4 Matthew 4:1–11; Mark 1:12–13; Luke 4:1–13.
5 Matthew 6:13.
6 Romans 13:11–14.
7 Matthew 17:14–21.
8 Matthew 10:1.
9 Luke 10:17–20.

Chapter 11

1   He is the 'prince of this world' (John 12:31; 14:30; 16:11), the 'God of this age' (2 Corinthians 4:4), and the 'prince and power of the air' (Ephesians 2:2, ESV). 'The whole world is under the control of the evil one' (1 John 5:19).
2   Acts 5:29.
3   See 2 Corinthians 11:16–33.
4   2 Timothy 3:12.
5   Daniel 3:16–18.

Chapter 12

1   Psalm 34:18.
2   Hebrews 13:5; 1 John 4:4.

Chapter 13

1   1 John 3:8.
2   John 12:31; 16:11.
3   Hebrews 2:14–15.
4   Matthew 12:29.

Chapter 14

1   John 14:12.
2   Matthew 14:25–29.
3   Ephesians 6:10.

Chapter 15

1 Matthew 5:3.

Chapter 165

1 Matthew 13:58.
2 Matthew 17:19–21.
3 Matthew 17:17.
4 Mark 11:22–24.
5 James 1:6–8.
6 Ephesians 3:20.

Chapter 17

1 Luke 18:1–8.
2 Matthew 7:7–8; John 14:14.
3 Matthew 16:17–19; 18:18.
4 Matthew 18:19–20.

Chapter 19

1 2 Timothy 4:18.
2 1 John 5:18.
3 Galatians 6:9.
4 James 4:7–8.

Chapter 20

1 1 Timothy 1:18; 6:12; 2 Timothy 2:3.
2 2 Corinthians 10:3–5.
3 Ephesians 6:10–18.

4 Ephesians 6:16; 1 Peter 1:5.
5 Matthew 26:41.
6 James 5:16.
7 Acts 16:25–26.
8 2 Chronicles 20:12, 21–22.
9 Ephesians 6:17.
10 Hebrews 4:12.
11 John 16:13.
12 Matthew 4:1–11; Mark 1:12–13; Luke 4:1–13.
13 Joshua 1:8.
14 Hebrews 10:25.
15 James 4:7.

Chapter 21

1 The story above includes quotes from Genesis 3:15; 6:5, slightly adapted; Colossians 2:15, slightly adapted; 1:13; Revelation 20:1–3, 7–10; and Matthew 25:41.
2 Revelation 20: 1–3.
3 Revelation 20:7–10.
4 Revelation 20:15.
5 Revelation 2:4.
6 Revelation 2:5.
7 Revelation 12:10–12.